The Counterrevolution

By

Edward C. Harwood

The Counterrevolution

By Edward C. Harwood

Copyright 2019, 1956, 1952, 1951 American Institute for Economic

Research, Creative Commons Attribution International 4.0

ISBN 978-0-913610-71-8

The Counterrevolution

By

Edward C. Harwood

AIER | AMERICAN INSTITUTE
for ECONOMIC RESEARCH

Contents

Acknowledgments

(1951)

THE MEMBERS of the editorial staff who wrote or assisted in preparing the material included in this publication were John J. Carter, Leonard H. Lempert, Edmund A. Mennis, and the undersigned. When the articles were originally published as editorial matter in the Research Reports, no attempt was made to give individuals credit for their respective contributions. However, in this library edition of the collected articles, I feel that the assistance of those indicated above should be acknowledged, because their research and critical analytical work were major factors in making publication in a more permanent form desirable.

— E. C. Harwood

Preface

ONE OF MY EARLIEST MEMORIES is of my father, Edward Crosby Harwood, in his khakis writing at his desk amid an orderly spread of other writings. A framed likeness of some grim Englishman hung on the opposite wall. When I asked him who that was, he smiled and said, "George Washington, an important man in the founding of America, and its first President." I later learned that Washington was also responsible for the selection in 1779 of West Point for his headquarters, which in 1802 became the United States Military Academy.

As a 1920 graduate of that famous academy, Harwood had taken the commissioned officer's solemn oath to: "...support and defend the Constitution of the United States against all enemies, foreign and domestic; that I will bear true faith and allegiance to the same; that I take this obligation freely, without any mental reservation or purpose of evasion; and that I will well and faithfully execute the duties of the office on which I am about to enter...."

Note well that the oath does not bind the officer to a President or other division of government or party, but to the Constitution, which distinction mattered when over the years military and civilian administrations attempted to suppress Harwood's developing economic and public-policy views. During his distinguished military career, Harwood served for more than four decades over two periods as well as serving in both the European and Pacific theaters in WWII, achieving the rank of Colonel and receiving the Bronze Star and the Legion of Merit. A biographical sketch of his life can be found in AIER's "E.C. Harwood – A Biographical Sketch" (Delay 2018).

Military life between world conflicts left much time for studies, which stimulated his interests in economics, the history of human endeavor, and what political conditions had retarded or fostered material progress. He had an early and abiding appreciation for how the American Revolution and the subsequent deliberations of the Founders and a young nation ultimately led to the Constitution and its Bill of Rights, unleashing the individual productivity of a people free to pursue their own best interests, to retain the results of their efforts, and to so build an economy previously unknown on earth.

His economic and financial studies and his considerable civil and military engineering and logistics talents led him into economic research. He soon became a published pioneer in the analyses of money and credit, even successfully predicting in 1929 that the expansive monetary policy of the 1920s would lead to a sudden correction, which calamity became known as The Great Depression.

His success as an economic analyst specializing in the causes of business cycles soon provided sufficient material for his book, "Cause and Control of the Business Cycle," which in 1932 and amid continuing economic and political drama, drew a recommendation from The Book of the Month Club.

The Depression sparked much international governance and economic policy discussion that Harwood in a series of correspondences and articles warned could be counterproductive, and could start a counterrevolution or retrogression from the successes of a people freed from thousands of years of arbitrary rule by monarchs, by state religions, and by sundry historic despots.

Realizing that much more research would be required to provide for a sorting of the ill-considered economic policy of the day, while teaching Military Science at MIT and with the encouragement of Vannevar Bush, Dean of the MIT School of Engineering, Harwood in 1933 organized the present American Institute for Economic Research as an apolitical, non-commercial, independent, scientific, and nonprofit organization that continues in Great Barrington, Massachusetts. Its 85 years of economic research and international policy analysis has been an effort to preserve for the citizen the best of that inherited from the past while assisting in wisely building for the future.

That labor proved challenging as the economic tinkering and experiments with socialist and populist national policy floundered until the immense effort of World War II conscripted all available men, money, and materials for the war effort. Indeed, the short-run demands of the Depression and the expense of war greatly complicated national economic policy, leading the AIER staff and Harwood to succinctly explain in successive and at times controversial "Research Reports" the continuing harm of shortsighted, inflationary monetary and national policies. Those reports soon provided sufficient material to become this 1951 book, "The Counterrevolution – American Foreign and Domestic Policy and Economic Aspects of National Defense," just as preparations for the Korean Conflict promised to further compromise American foundational principles with imprudent monetary and foreign policy.

Compiled into thirteen chapters, this book sketches those developments that led to the advances of Western Civilization by fostering the spread of individual freedoms, assesses the many social and governance issues of the first half of the Twentieth Century, and explains why those problematical issues constituted a counterrevolution as succinctly expressed in Patrick Henry's warning: "The Constitution is not a document for the government to restrain the people, it is an instrument for the people to restrain the government—lest it come to dominate our lives and interests."

Readers of this book will find much that is similar to present controversial economic and public policy matters. By republishing this book AIER hopes to help today's citizens better understand the continuing counterrevolutionary erosion of their Constitutional rights so famously won 235 years ago by lovers of independence and freedom and by founding patriots such as General Washington.

— Frederick Crosby Harwood

Foreword

The Great Revolution and the Quest for Pure Freedom

Edward Peter Stringham

(American Institute for Economic Research)

"The struggle against communism is a crucial one for the survival of Western Civilization." — (p.5) Edward C. Harwood

BY THE MIDDLE of the 20th-century, communism and various forms of socialism were expanding and controlled nearly half the world. Even France and England were nationalizing industries. This trend set off many alarm bells. Many cold warriors wanted to build up the size of the American government to be able to stand up to the communists. Many wanted to directly or indirectly engage the communists militarily. Many wanted active American government involvement with economies around the world through a series of Marshall Plans. The days of laissez-faire might be gone forever.

In 1951 Edward C. Harwood's *The Counterrevolution* made a clarion call that America not abandon the laissez-faire policies that made it great. To Harwood the antidote to expanding government around the world is not more government. We must stick to the principles of liberty here first and foremost. We must be the paragon and the best way to do that is to have strong markets. To Harwood, the ultimate battle is over ideas and leading by example. Harwood (p.74) concludes *The Counterrevolution* with, "In order to preserve and defend the United States during the foreseeable future, the path toward economic freedom must be regained. Public attention should be focused on the ways and means of restoring and preserving the circumstances that have made this country great. Much effort will be required, hard work, clear thought, and accurate scientific analysis." He writes, "If Western Civilization, the hope of mankind, is to be saved, it will not be through our bounty but by our example."(p.74) We should stick with the principles of laissez-faire at home and abroad.

Harwood makes the case that freedom is important for a few reasons. To Harwood, freedom attributes "worth and dignity to the individual man." (p.5) Freedom allows individuals to plan and choose their goals, gives all equal opportunity to pursue those goals, and lets individuals retain the fruits of their labor. Freedom of religion and freedom of thought matter too. To Harwood, the expansion of intellectual freedom in the Enlightenment encouraged advances in scientific knowledge. That, in turn, led to advances in technological progress which "rose like a giant from sleep to aid the wealth-producing activities of men." Harwood (p.21) writes, "Only men whose minds are free to pursue any subject and whose hands are free to produce any product could be expected to contribute so greatly to the accumulation of knowledge and to the creation of so large a variety of goods and services." So the development of freedom made the modern world possible.

To Harwood (p.18) Enlightenment thinkers advanced our thinking about liberty in many ways: "Shakespeare, Cervantes, Moliere, Milton, Dryden, Bacon, Spinoza, Leibnitz, Pascal, Locke, Rousseau, Paine, Voltaire, Montesquieu, Hume, Burke, and Adam Smith are but a few of those who wrote of the religious independence, social rights, and economic privileges that men of Western enjoy today." Harwood (p.19) highlights Locke's discussion of the importance of private property, Smith's discussion of the importance of free markets, and "finally, Thomas Paine's Common Sense" which "united the American Colonists in their struggle for freedom." He states that "here in America, conditions were propitious for a civilization based on freedom." Harwood (p.20) characterizes movements toward more freedom as the great revolution and it "reached a 'high water mark' near the end of the eighteenth century."

Despite the movements toward freedom, he says "There is little question that the goal of perfect freedom has not yet been attained," (p.22). He describes how the early industrial societies like England and America lacked a pure free-market and that led to various distortions and lack of opportunity for many. He says the inadequate freedom disinherited "a substantial portion of a nation's citizens" and denied equal opportunities. People are right to complain about that. But to Harwood, many people were missing out on the benefits of markets and the solution is to extend freedom to more people. The problems "are attributable to inadequate freedom and not to freedom itself" (p.25).

Unfortunately, however, many people look at problems in society and argue for a retreat against freedom. He describes movements against freedom as the counterrevolution and writes (p.8), "The counterrevolution is in progress throughout the world. It is recognized as communism; but fascism, various Socialist governments, the New Deal, and the Welfare State all have grown from the same roots." He says, "Karl Marx and his followers on the continent of Europe and the Fabian Society in England became the leaders of the counterrevolution," (p.24).

Harwood presents three alternatives. The first is to join the counterrevolution and he certainly does not advocate that. But he points out that our foreign policy is giving aid to governments that are part of the counterrevolution and here he refers to "the Socialist governments in England and France" (p.10). A second option is to simply push for the status quo and he does not advocate that either. He points out that communism was popular because of the various distortions in society. He says that preserving the status quo would become "increasingly costly and increasingly difficult as years pass (p.11). We have already diverged from economic freedom too much and that is lessening our industrial superiority and making us more vulnerable to attacks from Russia or elsewhere.

Harwood concludes that "Only the third course, to oppose communism by pressing on towards the goals of the great revolution within Western Civilization, appears to be a practical means of coping with the counterrevolution." We must reexamine the principles that made us great. He says, "The United States has become a great nation, a tower of industrial strength in the vanguard of Western Civilization, primarily because the goals of the great revolution were more nearly approached here than they were in Europe," (p.12). He says that we must reorient ourselves toward the principles we have stood for and then "encourage other nations to follow" (p.13). Harwood talks about getting rid of price controls, subsidies, high taxes, and other government interventions. He says, "Restoration of free markets is essential."

The critical takeaway here is to revise the way we perceive the broad historical narrative from the ancient world to the present. The dominant model of social management has been authoritarian control. It was the advent of freedom that constituted the revolution that transformed life for the human population. The counterrevolution, in this case, is not an embrace of progress but the opposite: a throwback to the days when people couldn't choose, couldn't broadly participate in commerce, couldn't enjoy material progress in their lifetimes. In Harwood's view, then, and a view I share, the way forward for America and the whole of civilization is to reject the counterrevolutionary model and continue the great revolution to realize freedom more perfect.

Introduction

DURING THE DECADES bracketing the arrival of the 20th century, the United States was a graveyard for successive waves of the revolutionary vanguard. Collectivist economic philosophies — including but not limited to communism, socialism, syndicalism, and fascism, with a heavy preponderance of the former two — arrived on American shores transmitted by books, pamphlets, and fiery orators. Yet each and every one found scant purchase and was rendered stillborn in short order.

So regular and definitive were the thwarting of communist and socialist proselytizing in America that they eventually called the very underpinnings of Marxist theory into question. An industrial power with millions of workers should, so the narrative went, be especially receptive to the establishment of a radical labor movement. As late as 1907, August Bebel of the German Social Democrats proclaimed that "Americans [would] be the first to usher in a Socialist republic." And while one year before Bebel's proclamation (one he would continue to make for some years) the sociologist Werner Sombart had already expressed exasperation with the publication of *Why Is There No Socialism in the United States?*, the Bolshevik revolution in Russia — an extremely unlikely place for the seeds of the worldwide socialist takeover to begin, at least according to Marxist dogma — turned attention away from the young, worker-rich, yet oddly revolution-averse North American nation.

Even during the Great Depression, when unemployment spiked to an estimated 25 percent in 1933 and GDP dropped by some 50 percent during the first five years, communist and socialist organizations saw a surge in membership, but never one that approached a groundswell.

Numerous explanations for the inability of collectivism to gain a foothold in the U.S. have been offered. Among Marxists, some are philosophically self-referential, such as dismissing Americans as lacking in "class consciousness". Others are somewhat thoughtful, such as those focusing upon the United States' being similar to (indeed, surpassing) England and Germany in its degree of industrialization but without the freighting of post-feudal cultural mores. The political structure in the United States, given its institutional inhospitality to third party and fringe political movements (via federalism and the electoral college), is at least a contributing factor. But a lack of effort was never blamed, nor should it have been: whether targeting labor, farmers, the poor, intellectuals, egalitarians, or the changing-but-ubiquitous throngs of the disenfranchised, international collectivist organizers have had the United States in the crosshairs for decades; America has stolidly resisted all of them.

* * *

In May 2018, the University of Chicago released the results of its most recent GenForward Survey, meant to gauge the political and economic leanings of a national group of Americans aged 18 to 34. Among this group, known today as millennials, 62 percent indicated thinking that a "strong government [is required] to handle today's complex economic problems." Of those identifying as Democrats, 61 percent indicated that they view socialism positively, as did 25 percent of those identifying as Republicans.

While one demographic group (much less a single poll) does not signal a Far Left revolt, the recent rise to national prominence among several avowedly socialist politicians in American politics is surprising. Over 2 million Americans voted for Senator Bernie Sanders (D-VT) in 2016 in his campaign for the Democratic presidential nomination, a candidate whose platform, in additional to the standard raft of welfarist proposals, included a new government railroad system (explicitly intended, in part, to take trucks off of roads) and the forcible breakup of large firms.

Also surprising is the widening embrace of massive government programs among average Americans: a Green New Deal, Medicare for

All, a universal basic income, a jobs guarantee, "free" college, and others. So, too, is the incremental embracing of collectivist speech among American officeholders, perhaps nowhere greater evidenced than by former President Barack Obama's attack on the concept of the self-made man and individual responsibility: "If you've got a business — you didn't build that." (Obama reversed himself four days later: "Of course Americans build their own businesses.")

American exceptionalism as a philosophy is alive and well; perhaps that is why it's so easy for so many to dismiss the notion that socialism is utterly impracticable and inevitably leads to totalitarianism and economic ruin. The insistence after each great failure of collectivist economics that "it wasn't really socialism" is likely believable by some Americans; it would not be surprising to find, as sidecar to that, that many more believe that the fabled pluck and ingenuity of American know-how could finally get it *right*. That such a system finally made workable would ostensibly free them from the never-ending scourge of living expenses, housing costs, college tuition, medical bills, and other mainstays of economic life can only be seen as sweetening the deal. But this is a heady place where costs are abstract. When they, on some rare occasion, become concrete, they're either kicked down the road or paid for by someone else. In any case, the proposals are viewed less as revolutionary than as what was right and salutary all along.

So when did the change take place?

While there is no V-shaped point of inflection, a focus upon the emergence of the United States from World War I seems to offer some explanations and evidence. The roots of the modern dalliance with collectivism, however currently expressed, lie less in left or right than in trusting big government. The New Deal, World War II, the Marshall Plan, the Space Race, the New Society, the S&L bailout, TARP, and other big government programs have cropped up in conjunction not only with the slow but steady erosion of the traditional American distrust in state largesse, but with low quality (indeed, often nonexistent) economic education and years of an undeterred expansion of entitlements.

* * *

We know now that communism never got out of second gear in the Soviet Union and that China ultimately came to embrace markets. Yet statism — the soul of the counterrevolution — has proceeded at an accelerating pace domestically: Americans face an exploding national debt and mounting annual budget deficits, and 1 dollar from Colonel Harwood's pocket at the time of the original publication of *The Counterrevolution* would purchase what it takes over 10 dollars to, today. A government that once held that individuals were overwhelmingly responsible for their personal conduct and fortunes has grown into a behemoth that deigns to tell us what food, drink, and substances we can ingest. Taxes are levied on everything from fruit bought from a vending machine vs. at a store (California) to soft drinks (Chicago) to selling and licensing performing rights for music (North Dakota). And once taken, these funds are handled in as irresponsible a way as can be imagined: in 2014 alone, the U.S. government misspent or lost over $125 billion of taxpayer monies.

The first coup of Harwood's *The Counterrevolution* is the title: while collectivists (in particular, on the left) have so long identified their initiatives in association with the term *revolutionary*, little could be further from the truth. As Lord Acton once commented in his notes, "The object of 'Revolution' is the prevention of revolution" — an exquisitely insightful comment, to say the least.

For compared to the hundreds of thousands of years of human existence in which subsistence-level existence was the default state, the last 250 years — a veritable blink of the eye, cosmically speaking — represents such a point of inflection in standards of living, longevity, infant mortality, and nearly every other measure of quality of life as to make the overwhelming majority of time humans have spent on earth inconceivable. Despite the screeds and slogans of would-be central planners and opponents of private property, individual liberty and steadily rising prosperity were — and remain — the true revolution.

In the opening chapter — "The Counterrevolution" — Colonel Harwood lays the situation before the reader, in terms and scenarios that are disconcertingly recognizable today: "The struggle against communism is not an attempt either to destroy Russia or to preserve the United States; it is … one for the survival of Western Civilization."

It is indeed. One wonders whether Harwood would be surprised or nonplussed to find that, looking forward five decades, the Soviet Union collapsed, essentially bloodlessly, in 1991, yet other collectivist states including Cuba, North Korea, Venezuela, and others, endure. Or that despite the failures evidenced by the Soviet Union — many of which came to light only after its collapse — the counterrevolution of which he wrote not only persists but has become more heated domestically with self-proclaimed socialists (often beneath its fashionable new pallium, 'Democratic Socialism') occupying U. S. government offices from mayoralties to Congress.

In chapters 2 and 3, Harwood gives an overview of the development of individual liberty, encapsulating the profound march of progress made by Western civilization: ideas building upon ideas starting with the Greeks, continuing into the Renaissance and the Age of Enlightenment, and finding their fullest realization in the New World, as the American revolutionaries memorialized it within the Declaration of Independence.

During the 19th century, economic development within the United States and England began, owing to several important distinctions — some cultural, some resource-based — to take on the dimensions of a controlled experiment, with collectivist ideas taking root earlier, and arguably to a greater extent, in England than in the U.S.

Individual freedom and land reform, a particularly striking example of Harwood's warning against the power of entrenched privilege or monopoly (using Denmark and New Zealand as historical examples), is the topic of the fourth chapter. The fifth chapter, "American Policy in the Short Run," puts forth the notion that while the fight against the counterrevolution is one to be fought on the scale of years and decades, in the short term an "idea offensive" can be mounted to thwart and reverse the tide of public opinion. The significance of the place the United States holds in the development of the foundational ideas in Western civilization should be a key part of that idea offensive; ideally, it would be common knowledge.

The seven following chapters constitute the bulk of the author's thesis. In chapters 6, 7, and 8 — "Economic Aspects of National Defense,"

"Basis of Plans for National Defense," and "Importance of Other Land Areas" — Harwood sanguinely assesses the difficulties inherent in coming up with a grand strategy for protecting the mainland of the United States. Citing the reasons why predicting what an enemy will do is difficult, not least of which being that technological evolution plays a major role in dictating both offensive and defensive capabilities, Harwood advises embracing a doctrine of flexibility. He also tempers dire predictions about the likelihood of an impending Russian invasion and reminds the reader that regardless of treaties or pacts, nations will in conflict and peace act primarily in their own best interest.

The subsequent four chapters cover specific aspects of Harwood's grand strategic vision.

Chapter 9, "Strength of our Armed Forces," deals with the tension between keeping a well-trained standing army and the characteristic inefficiencies — and in the event of a major deployment, the loss to industrial productivity — that such often implies. "Early Warning and New Weapons," chapter 10, describes the need to keep up with the development of new innovations in military technology abroad, with the caveat that a rapid, dynamic response to hostilities may trump the nominal superiority of certain enemy weapons systems and capabilities.

In chapters 11 and 12, "Industrial Capacity and National Defense" and "Choosing Wisely Among National Resources," Colonel Harwood compares industrial production of the United States with that of its allies and enemies, concluding that decisive factors in any upcoming conventional war will include the ability to convert peacetime to wartime production quickly and efficiently, the productivity of the industrial workforce, and maintaining current levels of industrial capacity (total output). The latter, he notes, is not exclusively a matter of automation, mechanization, or applied science: government policies that are not explicitly collectivist but nevertheless erode the primacy of property rights often play a pivotal role in the incremental erosion of manufacturing strength, and thus national defense.

A brief conversation about the opportunity costs of such recent initiatives as Social Security, farm supports, and unemployment insurance rounds out this chapter. Harwood notes that Americans "should be concerned with the day-to-day choices among alternative uses of land, labor, and capital ... if possible improving the circumstances that have made great progress possible."

Lastly, in "Our Greatest Threat," Harwood states his conviction that what fundamentally imperils the national security of the United States is the inability to "differentiate between measures that increase and ... decrease economic freedom," resulting both in the misuse and dissipation of real resources and in forgone opportunities. The path back will not be won, the colonel warns, by massive state programs or philosophical gymnastics, but by hard work accompanied by a concerted effort to rekindle the philosophical flame of our material improvement.

★ ★ ★

As a final note, Edward C. Harwood was a graduate of the United States Military Academy at West Point; I am as well, albeit having tossed my cap some 75 years after him.

One of many traditions transcending generations of USMA graduates is memorization of the Bishop Shipman poem "The Corps," which one inevitably remembers for the entirety of their life. Near the end, the author writes:

> The Long Grey Line of us stretches
> Through the years of a century told
> And the last man feels to his marrow
> The grip of your far-off hold
> Grip hands with us now, though we see not[.]

While we swear an oath to uphold the common defense, that stipulation is — for logical and historical reasons — overwhelmingly assumed to mean on the field of battle. Even before graduating from West Point, I had somewhat iconoclastically come to view the role of West Pointers in the defense of the United States within a far-broader context: one in which all but purely defensive military conflict is overwhelmingly deleterious to the nation, in which the stringent defense of the individual and private property is the approach to governance most consistent with upholding and defending liberty, and in which the increase in the size and scope of the U.S.

government, especially since World War I, has been egregiously at odds with the founding principles.

As a fellow grad, I felt Sherwood's gripping of hands with Colonel Harwood: not only in reading this manuscript but in working under the auspices of the American Institute for Economic Research, the institution which he founded. And I am reminded that there have always been those among the Long Gray Line who see the struggle for liberty in terms vastly beyond taxpayer-financed expeditions to foreign battlefields.

The counterrevolution proceeds; we true revolutionaries have our work cut out for us.

— Peter C. Earle

The Counterrevolution

THE STRUGGLE against communism is not an attempt either to destroy Russia or to preserve the United States; it is not merely another of the numerous rivalries between nations that have crowded the pages of history. The struggle against communism is a crucial one for the survival of Western Civilization. Whether this struggle will mark the decline and fall of Western Civilization or will set the stage for a new, great advance comparable to that of recent centuries remains to be seen.

Because this is not merely a struggle between jealous or greedy monarchs nor solely a war for empire and trade nor a religious war between ignorant and intolerant tribesmen, we must seek below the surface and behind events of the day for the fundamental causes of the conflict within Western Civilization. At least briefly we must sketch the outline of developments on a broad front and in the perspective of recent centuries.

The Situation in Perspective

Several hundred years ago Western Civilization consisted of many vast feudal estates, innumerable peasant holdings of small farms, uncounted villages, and towns, and a few cities, small by today's standards. For the most part, men lived as their fathers and grandfathers before them had lived; folklore and superstition were generally considered the intellectual keys to understanding, and scientific knowledge as we think of it

1

today was almost unheard of; class distinctions were rigid in many parts of the civilized world; village industry was controlled by the guilds and other authorities; progress was not generally expected and often was not toler- ated; most men were slaves, seemingly held in perpetual bondage by cus- tom, fear, ignorance, and superstition. Only the more fortunate who had been granted dominion over the earth and the fruits thereof, seemingly by an inscrutable providence, could live much differently than did beasts of burden in that almost-forgotten age.

Nevertheless, within that civilization, an idea began to find increas- ing acceptance. In a word, this was the idea that individuals might be free; but its scope developed gradually, and even today we are not sure that we grasp its full implications.[1]

Aided by many circumstances that need not be described in detail, this idea of freedom found more and more disciples. It attributed worth and dignity to the individual man; and, as men gradually and almost reluctantly accepted this new idea, they likewise accepted many increased responsibili- ties that fostered individual growth in countless ways.

Intellectual freedom opened the doors of the new frontiers of science. As a result, technological progress rose like a giant from sleep to aid the wealth-producing activities of men. Here in America circumstances were most propitious for a civilization based on the idea of freedom. The results we are familiar with; but the magnitude of them is sometimes overlooked because to us they have become commonplace.

Freedom found acceptance in parts of Europe also. Major social changes marked its advent, and great material progress was one result. However, in much of that area, the great revolution never was so suc- cessful as it was in the United States. Apparently, in only two countries of

---

1 One suggestion is that men are free to the extent that the culture or society in which they live permits them to plan and choose their goals, provides equality of opportunity to act effectively in pursuit of those goals, and permits them to retain the fruits of their labors. Throughout this report we shall use "freedom" as a blanket label for these circumstances and such others as may be necessary to constitute optimum circumstances for the economic welfare of men in society. We realize that such use of a term is loose characterization rather than scientifically accurate specification or naming, but it will serve the purpose here.

Europe, Denmark, and Switzerland, has the great revolution maintained its gains or progressed in recent decades.

Even here in the United States, however, complete freedom was not reached. Conditions here differed greatly in many respects from those in the Old World; but we now realize that various laws and customs carried over from the Old World had the effect of denying freedom, at least in some degree, to many of the people of our own Nation.

The results of imperfect or partial freedom were not all good. Great material progress came, but the greatly increased production of wealth was not equitably distributed to those who produced it. As a result, 12- and 14-hour days for women and children were common in the factories of England, more extensive and more degrading poverty pervaded the slums of Europe, and urban and rural slums developed in the United States.

So striking did the increasing maldistribution of wealth become that many men abandoned the battle for freedom and turned back; thus the counterrevolution within Western Civilization was born. For the past hundred years, the counterrevolution has been gaining strength. Its basic ideas were developed earlier by the Utopian Socialists and were organized as counter revolutionary doctrine by Karl Marx and his followers. These ideas are the roots from which modern communism, socialism, fascism, the New Deal, and the Welfare State all have grown.

In Russia the counterrevolution has reached the apparently inevitable goal; a new despotism has replaced the old. In this fact, there is a lesson for all who desire to learn it. Marx and Engels predicted success for communism (the militant branch of socialism) first in the great industrialized nations where they expected the proletariat to unite and cast off its chains. But communism succeeded first, not in the more advanced industrial nations, but in Russia, where the progress of the great revolution had been retarded. The reason is not difficult to understand. The counterrevolution is fundamentally a retreat from individual freedom, from responsibility and authority for each individual to the sheltering arms of an all-powerful state. Naturally, communism succeeded first where the progress of the great revolution had been least; and it still achieves success most readily in the backward nations of the world, where the substitution of a new despotism for the old is relatively easy.

The Source of Communism's Strength

However, the fact that communism succeeded first in Russia and that it gains ground most rapidly in the more backward nations of the world should not be permitted to encourage a false sense of security. The basic principles of communism have been widely accepted; and the counter-revolution has gained strength during the past century in nearly all nations of Western Civilization, including our own. In order to grasp the significance of these gains, we must first understand the source of the strength of communism.

Although the hopes it offers are known by many to be illusory and although its promises are vain, communism derives its strength from those who, because of the inequitable distribution of incomes, have become the underprivileged of all lands. What other hope have those who are denied a substantial part of the fruits of their labor (in order that the perquisites of the privileged may be preserved) than that someone will somehow redistribute currently produced wealth in accordance with men's needs? The Marxian slogan, "From each according to his abilities; to each according to his needs," offers to the poor, hope comparable to the hope of a better world offered by many religions. Communism has the added advantage of promising to provide in this world now or in the immediate future what some religions offer only in the next world at some future time.

The strength of communism's appeal results from its promise to eliminate special privilege for the few and the inevitably corresponding inequality of opportunity and obvious inequity of reward for the many. Communism has grown in strength as special privilege has grown; the farther the nations of Western Civilization have departed from equality of opportunity, one ingredient of freedom, the more they have drifted toward communism.

Fascism often is discussed as though it were the opposite of communism, but such is not precisely the case. Hitler, Mussolini, and Stalin were different in many respects; but the principles of their economic ideologies were the principles of socialism; their initial appeal was to the underprivileged; and the final result, a new despotism, was the same in all three instances.

Summary of the Present Situation

In view of the foregoing, we may summarize the present situation somewhat as follows: Western Civilization as we know it today is the outcome of a great revolution that followed the acceptance of new ideas and that accompanied the progress toward individual freedom including equality of opportunity and economic justice[2] for all men. However, virtually complete freedom as herein described has not yet been reached except in relatively small areas of the world and even there only for brief periods.

Perhaps primarily because we of this civilization have stopped short of the goal, the results have in part been an inequitable distribution of currently produced wealth. In the minds of many, not even the material progress made possible by the great revolution can offset results that seem so evil. Either not realizing that the goal had never been reached or not understanding that the evils they deplored were attributable to imperfect freedom, many leaders in thought and action sought to turn back; thus the counterrevolution was born.

The counterrevolution is in progress throughout the world. It is recognized as communism; but fascism, various Socialist governments, the New Deal, and the Welfare State all have grown from the same roots.

Such is the situation in this midpoint of the twentieth century. American foreign policy, if it is to be successful in the long run, must cope with the counterrevolution in Western Civilization.

---

2 Economic justice refers to the third part of the definition of freedom previously given. Men who are free to plan and choose their goals and who enjoy equality of opportunities to seek their goals may be said to receive economic justice if they are permitted to retain the fruits of their labors.

Lesson of the Immediate Past

Before proceeding to a discussion of American foreign policy, a brief review of recent developments will be helpful. A valuable lesson can be learned from mistakes of the recent past.

Germany and Russia were enemies in World War II, not because their ideologies differed, but because there was not room on the same continent for their ambitious rulers. We were allied with Russia, not because Russia was one of the democracies fighting for freedom, but because Russia happened to be fighting Germany and could be induced to fight Japan.

However, Americans are sometimes thought by their political leaders to be squeamish and unwilling to face the facts of life. Consequently, the wartime administration sought to "sell" the American people the notion that Stalin was a respectable companion in arms. They were not content to use him to the extent that he was useful, while keeping in mind that he was the leader of the counterrevolution threatening Western Civilization: they insisted on adopting Russia into the family of peace-loving nations. In our preoccupation with winning World War II, the Nation's leaders apparently closed their eyes to the important long-term developments that have been described here.

Our foreign policy during and immediately after World War II was a series of blunders precisely because we dealt with successive short-term situations as though there were no long-run fundamental conflicts of aims or as though we were blind to other than immediate pressing developments. Such was our major error, and the lesson should not be forgotten.

What Must Our Foreign Policy Provide For?

Prior to World War II, American foreign policy had to cope with two classes of potential enemies. The first included Germany and Japan as potential enemies for the same reason, ambition for power, that nations have so often been enemies since the dawn of recorded history. The other class of potential enemies may be roughly designated communists or, to be more specific, the counterrevolutionary elements within Western Civilization.

Fortunately, the problem of formulating an adequate foreign policy is simplified in some respects by the fact that, in coping with Russia as our only potential enemy of substantial strength in the first class (having a ruler whose ambitions for more territory and power make him a potential enemy), we shall be coping to some extent with the world-wide counter-revolutionary movement.

On the other hand, the situation is complicated by the fact that, in choosing a foreign policy intended to cope with Russia's ambitions for more territory and power, we may erroneously assume that the long-run problem of the counterrevolution is automatically solved merely because we associate the long-run problem also with Russia. Actually, the ruler of Russia is not the long-run problem: he is merely its temporary figurehead or symbol. Regardless of what happens to him or to Russia in the next several years, the long-run problem of the counterrevolution will remain.

What Can Be Done about Counterrevolution?

We now come to the question, "How can the foreign policy of one nation deal with counterrevolution within a civilization?" A nation faced with such a counterrevolution has any one of three courses available. Each of these will be discussed in turn.

The first possible course is to join the counterrevolution. To a far greater extent than many people realize, the United States already has chosen this course. Many internal policies, especially (but not by any means solely) some of those adopted in the past two decades, conform to the principles advocated by the counterrevolutionists. In our foreign policies also we have not hesitated to give extensive financial aid to the political parties in control of various governments that are aiding and abetting the counter-revolution. We refer to the Socialist governments of England and France.

It should be apparent that the first possible course, which we have already chosen in part, will be self-defeating in the long run. If we encourage the counterrevolution in other nations and yield to its wiles at home, we shall end by joining wholeheartedly, while Western Civilization declines and falls as others have done before.

The second possible course is to attempt to preserve the status quo, that is, neither to press on with the original revolution nor to join the counterrevolution. This apparently was an objective of the Truman policy. Although the Truman policy appeared to be somewhat inconsistent for several months, including as it did the extension of military aid to Greece and Turkey and the denial of military aid to Nationalist China and Korea, subsequent actions and announcements indicated that the policy had become firm. In essence, it appeared to contemplate preservation of the status quo as of June 1950 indefinitely.

The second course, preserving the status quo, would seem to us impossible if we may legitimately deduce from history something other than that men never learn anything from history. And, aside from the lessons of history, we know that the conditions in which communism is rooted and from which it derives its strength have become increasingly favorable to communism; this trend seems destined to continue until progress toward the goals of the great revolution is resumed. Preserving the status quo would become increasingly costly and increasingly difficult as the years pass. Such a policy is only a slower, not a less certain, road to destruction in the long run than the first possible course.

The third possible course is to oppose communism, but what effective means are there for opposing communism? An answer is not difficult to find if one remembers that communism is the ideology of the counterrevolution. Only if Western Civilization presses on toward the goals of the great revolution will the circumstances that have fostered the counterrevolution be changed. Only as the source of its strength is reduced and finally eliminated will the counterrevolution be weakened and finally defeated in the long run.

Practicable Foreign Policy

Only the third course, to oppose communism by pressing on toward the goals of the great revolution within Western Civilization, appears to be a practicable means of coping with the counter revolution.

Fortunately, no other great nation is as well prepared as our own to undertake this task. In order to reorient our aim, we should study again the

Declaration of Independence, the Constitution of the United States, the writings of Jefferson, and other documents, such as Lincoln's emancipation address, that have described the goals we once sought so eagerly. Then, we must ascertain why the goals have not been reached, why inequality of opportunity and an inequitable distribution of currently produced wealth became so marked even in the United States as well as in the rest of Western Civilization. Only then shall we be in a position to correct the fundamental errors in our procedures that have delayed progress toward the goals of the great revolution.

The United States has become a great nation, a tower of industrial strength in the vanguard of Western Civilization, primarily because the goals of the great revolution were more nearly approached here than they were in Europe. In the greater material progress here in the United States, we have all around us tangible evidence that should more than justify the faith needed to press on. Surely we of all peoples of the world should know that freedom for the individual (not merely freedom from outside domination for a nation), equality of opportunity, and economic justice are among the important goals to be sought.

Implementation of a Sound Foreign Policy

We have concluded that the only sound foreign policy for the United States in the long run is to resume our former place in the vanguard of the great revolution, to press on toward the goals of more nearly complete individual freedom, and to encourage other nations to follow. However, we shall be ill-prepared for such a position of leadership until we have reoriented the policies that we apply at home.

Too long have we yielded to the urgings of those who have joined the counterrevolution. Alger Hiss and others like him may not be traitors in the ordinary sense of that word, implying betrayal of their country in order to give advantage to a foreign enemy; perhaps they are merely miseducated men whose good intentions have led them to join the counterrevolution within Western Civilization. We shall underestimate the potential danger if we do not realize that such men are not misanthropic freaks but the legitimate products of some of the Nation's leading educational institutions.

Domestic Policy

Coping with the counterrevolution at home will not be easy. In order to regain the road toward the goals of the great revolution, we shall have to retrace some steps taken in recent years and turn aside from other goals toward which considerable progress has been made.

Specifically, corrective action will be needed along at least three general lines. First, the distortions of and interference with free-market relationships must be reduced as rapidly as possible and ultimately ended; second, all special privileges must be eliminated; and, third, the activities of the Federal Government must be reduced to the role of national defense and prevention of license or abuse of freedom.

Restoration of free markets is essential if progress is to be made toward the goals of the great revolution. If men are to choose wisely among possible economic alternatives, they must be free to buy and sell at prices agreed among themselves without government intervention, subsidies, or controls; they must be free to select, hold, and exchange the money or standard of value that they deem most suitable for the purpose (with men's customs and views as they are, the gold standard must be restored); and such abuses of the monetary system as inflation must be eliminated. For 35 years Government intervention and "management" of the Nation's money-credit mechanism have resulted in progressively greater distortions and more extreme interference with free markets. The counterrevolutionists throughout the world have long regarded inflation as their most potent weapon; and events in Russia, Germany, France, and elsewhere have confirmed their judgment.

Holders of special privileges, especially those related to monopolies of natural resources (including land), under existing customs and laws acquire, at the expense of the producers, an expanding portion of the wealth currently produced. This situation results in increasing the number of underprivileged members at the base of society from whom communism derives its voting strength (but not, of course, its intellectual "front"), and it diverts from producers some of the means that could be used to increase production. Because the situation in this respect is more acute in various other countries, for example, Italy, many observers see the problem there more clearly. Nevertheless, this problem is evident here in the United States and seems destined to become far more acute as the stimulating effects of prolonged inflation diminish.

Reduction of the role of the Federal Government to the national defense and to the function of umpire for the purpose of preventing license or abuse of the principles of freedom is essential to the efficiency of the Government in performing its primary functions. United States Senators, who should have time for analysis and study of important policy matters such as those described here, spend their valuable time bickering over the price support levels for Valencia peanuts and innumerable other trivialities that have become the day-to-day business of an elephantine bureaucracy. A republic need not be as inefficient as a totalitarian form of government that attempts to control all economic activities; but, if we continue adding to the functions of our Federal Government as we have during recent decades, the fundamental efficiency of free men functioning in free markets will be replaced by the lumbering and creaking performance of a vast bureaucracy. We shall then be as inefficient as our totalitarian enemies.

Foreign Policy

For the purpose of coping with the immediate threat resulting from Russia's ambitions for more territory and power, our short-term foreign policy may well be based on the expedient, for the time being, rather than on principle. If war with Russia is imminent, we should not scorn any allies, even one such as Spain. However, there is no need to repeat the silly process we went through when we used Russia as an ally in World War II; we need not fool ourselves that we are coping with the counterrevolution when we "make a deal" with men like Franco of Spain.

On the other hand, our intervention in Korea had no other excuse but as part of our long-run plan to cope with the counterrevolution. All of our military experts seem to be agreed that Korea would be a liability rather than an asset in the event of war with Russia in the near future. Obviously then, in Korea, we should have insisted on pressing the great revolution, on progress toward the goals of individual freedom, equality of opportunity, and economic justice for all men. Was there any other goal in Korea worth the life of a single American soldier? (Surely our battle cry in Korea should not have been, "Restore to the landlords their vast feudal estates!")

If in doubt as to how progress toward those goals can be made in Korea, we might well study the situation in Denmark and New Zealand. The lessons we should learn would have the added advantage that they could also be applied here in the United States when we finally realize how badly we need to apply them.

A National Policy Commission?

We realize that the policies we have suggested may not be generally accepted at first, The Nation's legislators who have been preoccupied with Valencia peanuts can hardly be expected to see world affairs in the perspective here described at first glance, and shallow or confused thinking about the problems of Western Civilization in the twentieth century is by no means confined solely to the halls of Congress. Therefore, we raise the following question: Has not the time come for selection of a National Commission on Foreign and Domestic Policy? Such a commission, composed of the most competent men who can be drawn to its service, could be expected to survey the entire problem of American foreign and domestic policy from a nonpolitical viewpoint. By holding extensive public hearings and exploring the various possibilities involved, public attention could be focused on these critical problems of our times, and the public could become informed regarding these matters. Finally, before its work ended, such a commission could be expected to report findings and recommendations concerning foreign and domestic policy much as the Constitutional Convention did in 1787 or as the National Monetary Commission did on a less extensive scale four decades ago.

Unless something like this is done, we greatly fear that the statue in New York Harbor of the goddess of liberty enlightening the world will no longer be an appropriate symbol of United States policy at home and abroad. And, in that event, what shall it profit us if we gain widespread dominion and for the time being stabilize the world if in so doing we lose our own principles? We shall gain nothing but a little temporary security and shall lose all that we treasure highly as the United States declines and falls with the rest of Western Civilization, a victim of the counterrevolution.

The Development of Individual Freedom

"MEN ARE FREE to the extent that the culture or society in which they live permits them to plan and choose their goals, provides equality of opportunity to act effectively in pursuit of those goals, and permits them to retain the fruits of their labors."[3]

Thus the degree of freedom for individuals depends on the customs, laws, and other cultural circumstances of the society in which they live. Changes in such circumstances may add to or subtract from the freedom of individuals; consequently, the individuals of one age are more or less free than those who lived before them. The history of freedom's development, therefore, is the history of certain cultural changes within society.

Early Societies

Individual members of early tribal societies were placed by the accident of birth in relatively rigid cultural molds. To a far greater extent than most of us can even imagine today, the individual was compelled to conform to the religious, political, economic, and social institutions of his tribe. Pervading the whole tribal culture was the influence of religion.

---

3 Individuals within a society may be *more* or *less* free but not free absolutely. All human societies of which we have any knowledge have restrained individuals, to some extent at least, in order to prevent license (abuse of freedom).c

The tribe's political leaders were assumed to be gods, in part at least, and to have inherited divine powers. "An individual did not join a church. He was born and reared in a community whose social unity, organization, and traditions were symbolized and celebrated in the rites, cults, and beliefs of a collective religion. Education was the induction of the young into community activities that were interwoven at every point with custom, legends, and ceremonies intimately connected with and sanctioned by a religion."[4]

The opportunities for individual choice of goals and means, for self-development, were severely restricted.

The Greeks

The historical record indicates that the first human society to offer its individual members an unusual degree of freedom was the Greek civilization during the five centuries prior to the birth of Christ. Although the Greeks had many gods, whose assumed whims governed to a large extent individuals, families, and the state, Greek religion served, rather than dominated, the state. Speculative thought and artistic creation were considered divine attributes that men might acquire.[5]

Although the Greeks became relatively free from the dictates of religious authority, the methods of religious inquiry were to some extent carried over into the field of natural philosophy. The philosophers, some of whom are still widely quoted, developed logic but depended for their premises on unaided perception and introspection to such an extent that their method virtually paralleled the religious method of acquiring knowledge by divine revelation. Thus Greek thought in its search for knowledge was limited by methods the restrictive effects of which have become apparent only as modern methods of scientific inquiry have been developed.

Nevertheless, within limits, the individual Greek enjoyed certain freedoms. If he was not a member of the slave class, he was able to participate in the democratic government of the city-state. Moreover, he was able to make valuable contributions to mathematics and physics; Archimedes'

---

4 "John Dewey, *Intelligence in the Modern World* (New York, The Modern Library, 1939), p. 1030.c

5 *Encyclopedia Britannica* Vol. 10, p. 850.c

Principle, for example, has been regarded by many as the first step in the science of mechanics.

The Dark Ages

The light of individual freedom that burned brightly in Greece was dimmed as the centuries passed, and the Golden Age became only a legend. Even the legend was unknown to most of those born in Western Civilization during the Dark Ages who found themselves in a society where rigid conformity to authority prevailed. "The law in the Middle Ages was not supposed to have been made by anyone, either an individual or a people. It was imagined to be as permanent and as unchangeable as anything in nature. Literally, all law was felt to be externally valid and to some degree sacred."[6]

As we have said before, most men were slaves, seemingly held in perpetual bondage by custom, fear, ignorance, and superstition.

The Renaissance

Gradually, individuals born into Western Civilization found an increasing range of choice among goals and more opportunities to pursue those goals. However, the road toward greater freedom led through many difficulties.

Although the crusades of the twelfth and thirteenth centuries may be thought of primarily as religious movements, they also broke "the shell of isolation which had encased the people of early medieval Europe."[7]

The religious, economic, political, and social customs of the Far East thus became direct common knowledge to many thousands of Europeans; and word of the Far East ultimately came back to the many more who had remained behind.

The development of freedom for individuals during the later Middle Ages and earlier stages of the Renaissance cannot be traced in detail here.

---

6 George H. Sabine, *A History of Political Theory* (New York, Henry Holt, and Company, 1937), p. 202.c

7 Curtiss P. Nettels, *The Roots of American Civilization* (New York, F. S. Crofts, and Company, 1938), p. 2.c

Every schoolboy has learned of the Magna Carta (1215) and the resulting limitation of the King's authority. The struggle against papal imperialism in France followed by the establishment of the Kingdom of France was another landmark on the road toward increased freedom for the individuals in Western Civilization.

Perhaps the development of greatest significance to the economic freedom of individuals was the Black Death. The bubonic plagues that ravaged Europe from 1347 to 1350 proved to be a blessing in strange disguise for those who survived and their progeny. For the first time in several centuries, unused but cultivable land became available throughout most of Europe. In spite of the edicts of kings elsewhere and numerous laws enacted by the Parliament in England, real wages generally rose rapidly, and the share of production taken by landlords declined in Western Civilization. Many millions who before had the opportunity only to obtain a bare subsistence by unremitting toil on the lord of the manor's land found others bidding for their services, other land available, and, in many instances, complete freedom from former ties that had been broken by the sudden deaths of landlords and masters.

To what extent the Renaissance can be attributed to the economic conditions that followed the Black Death may remain debatable. However, we do know that three centuries later historians looked back on the decades following the plagues as a second Golden Age.

From approximately 1400 through 1550 the arts and sciences revived. Furthermore, recovery and translation of Greek and Latin manuscripts, the invention of the printing press, and the great increase in exploration enabled men to expand the scope of their efforts. Roger Bacon, Leonardo da Vinci, Copernicus, and Christopher Columbus were among those who made best use of the new opportunities.

As men sought to explore the unknown, they soon began to question even the authority of the prevailing religion. That this religion should have been forced to relinquish its control over secular affairs was unusual; that its authority should be successfully questioned in its admitted realm of the spiritual and moral was unprecedented. Men had doubted before; but the inquisition, stake, and fire had been ruthlessly and apparently successfully used to maintain the authority of the accepted religion. For the first time in many centuries, men asserted their right to freedom of choice even among religions.

With the details of Martin Luther's and John Calvin's work, we are not here concerned. We need only note that by 1688 the principle of freedom of choice among religions had been established in important parts of Western Civilization.

The Transition from Natural Philosophy to Modern Science

In the early decades of the Renaissance, natural philosophy or the search for knowledge of this world leaned heavily on the translations from the works of Greek masters of speculative thought. Their authority influenced the Scholastics in their search for knowledge much as the papal authority of Rome influenced religious thought.

However, Francis Bacon argued effectively against dependence on the deductive reasoning of scholasticism and urged that inquiry be based on experience and experiment. The fruitfulness of the new approach was proven by such men as Vesalius in the study of anatomy, Galileo and Kepler in the physics and astronomy, and Boyle in his chemical research. Freedom from the bonds of authority thus gave men the opportunity to push scientific inquiry along new paths that have led to the great advances of our times.

Literature and Political Thought

As to science, so also to literature and political thought the Renaissance brought new life. Shakespeare, Cervantes, Moliere, Milton, Dryden, Bacon, Spinoza, Leibnitz, Pascal, Locke, Rousseau, Paine, Voltaire, Montesquieu, Hume, Burke, and Adam Smith are but a few of those who wrote of the religious tolerance, political independence, social rights, and economic privileges that men of Western Civilization enjoy today.

Milton's *Areopagitica* urged freedom for the press. Voltaire fought religious intolerance and extolled the virtues of representative government. Montesquieu's Spirit of the Laws suggested the separating of the legislative, executive, and judicial powers and the balancing of these powers against one another. Locke's *Two Treatises of Government* argued that governments exist in order to further liberty, to protect the property of individuals, to limit abuse and tyranny, and to abolish monopoly and privilege. Rousseau, in spite of the shortcomings of his reasoning and his social-contract and natural-rights theories, urged greater confidence in men as individuals responsible for their own destiny. Adam Smith's *The Wealth of Nations* championed free markets. And, finally, Thomas Paine's *Common Sense* united the American Colonists in their struggle for freedom.

The Individual in America

The discovery of the New World in 1492 was a major event in the development of liberty for individuals. Here in America, conditions were propitious for a civilization based on freedom. Of course, the freedom we think of was not obtained immediately. Customs and traditions of the Old were carried over into the Colonies. Gradually, however, the conditions of relatively free land, the demands of the new country on the initiative and resourcefulness of individuals, the religious toleration advocated by men such as Roger Williams, and the great distances separating the Colonists from the authority of the Old World led to a relatively great degree of liberty for those in America.

Finally, the Declaration of Independence asserted the new rights of men, and the new theory of the just society was given coherence and political form in the Constitution of the United States in 1787 and in the Bill of Rights in 1791.

Thus, infants born in the United States at the end of the eighteenth century found themselves in a society that differed greatly from that of their ancestors 500 years earlier. No longer did the cultural web of religious, political, economic, and social authority close nearly every avenue of individual development.

Religious authority, although important, no longer dominated men's lives. The church not only was severed officially from the state but also interests and values wholly unrelated to the church or religion were important influences on men's desires and aims.[8]

The authority of the state was no longer the whim of an individual or a group of individuals arbitrarily chosen or appointed. Through the representative form, men had gained control over the government of their society.

Authority over economic activities was lessened, and economic opportunities were greatly increased; indeed, an approach to equality of economic opportunities was achieved. The monopoly privileges and authority of the landlord were almost eliminated by the relatively abundant land available. Men were no longer restricted to the manor but could seek their own land and could obtain it at little or no cost. Moreover, the authority of masters also was largely eliminated. Although an apprenticeship was usually necessary in order to learn a trade, craftsmen thereafter were relatively free to apply their skills.

Finally, the life of the frontier tended to modify the social relationships that had prevailed in the Old World. Class distinctions virtually disappeared in the frontier settlements.

Conclusions

Looking backward, we now can see that the great revolution within Western Civilization reached a "high water mark" near the end of the eighteenth century. In the United States, the basic contract of government embodied the revolutionary notion that men should be free to choose their goals, have equal opportunities to pursue those goals, and be permitted to retain the fruits of their labors. This form of government presupposed that the worth and survival of a society of men depend on the quality of its individual members, that freedom thrusts responsibility upon men, and that men grow or develop to carry the responsibility they assume.

To a lesser extent, the principles of freedom had also been applied elsewhere within Western Civilization. Consequently, new hopes for mankind were widely accepted in the Old as well as the New World.

---

8 John Dewey, *op. cit.*, p. 1033.

The Revolt Against
Partial Freedom

THE RESULTS of the great material progress that has occurred in the United States in the nineteenth and twentieth centuries are not difficult to see. The factories, utilities, houses, railroads, radios, telephones, television sets, refrigerators, highways, farming equipment, and airplanes are but a small part of the evidence of material progress.

The contributions of individual freedom to this material progress have been manifold and immeasurably great. When men are permitted to plan and choose their goals, are provided an approach to equality of opportunity that aids them to act effectively in pursuit of those goals, and are permitted to retain the fruits of their labor, relatively greater production is virtually assured.

Permitting men to plan and choose their goals stimulates inquiry (the pursuit of knowledge) and encourages production. Enabling men to choose their own goals has stimulated men's imaginations and thus has encouraged new scientific discoveries, new inventions, new industries, and new methods that have characterized the technological advance. Only men whose minds are free to pursue any subject and whose hands are free to produce any product could be expected to contribute so greatly to the accumulation of knowledge and to the creation of so large a variety of goods and services.

Of course, permission to choose one's goals without equality of opportunity to pursue those goals would be of but limited value. The successes of many Americans would have been impossible in the absence of an approach to equality of opportunity. Great contributions to material progress in America have been made by persons who, under an all-powerful state, never would have had an opportunity to apply their talents.

The third aspect of individual freedom, permission to retain the one's labor, has been equally important in its contribution to material progress. The promise of an equitable reward provides an incentive for the original producer and others to continue their efforts; and, equally if not more important, the more capable producers thus have at their disposal increasing means that enable them to be even more productive.

Partial Freedom

Individual freedom has evolved gradually, and there is little question that the goal of perfect[9] freedom has not yet been attained. In varying degrees in various places, society prevents some of its members from choosing their goals, has failed in numerous instances to provide equality of opportunity, and has prevented some of its members from retaining the fruits of their labors.

In England the results of less than optimum freedom were striking. There the Industrial Revolution proceeded rapidly, aided by thousands of artisans and inventors who had fled from various countries of Europe in search of greater religious and political freedom. The production increased at a rate that seemed to promise ease and plenty for all that would not be far distant.

However, at the same time vast estates were increasing in number and size. Much of the commons (or common land) formerly available free or at nominal cost to villagers was enclosed and used only for sheep pastures, deer parks, and great hunting domains.

---

9 "Perfect" does not imply "absolute". An absolutely free man, living, is difficult even to imagine, except perhaps as a Robinson Crusoe on a forgotten island.

England's bold peasantry, the sturdy yeomen and their descendants, were forced off the land and became the disinherited proletariat of England's growing cities. They had no other alternative to accepting whatever wages were offered them than starving. Many did starve in "bad times," but at all times the pressure of those seeking work tended to reduce wages to the subsistence level. Supposedly free markets and noninterference by government with wages and prices, policies advocated most effectively by Adam Smith and his successors, increased the competition for jobs among the underprivileged. Among the privileged classes (who apparently never realized that special privileges for some and optimum freedom for all were incompatible) Malthus' theory of overpopulation seemed to provide a ready explanation of the "natural" and therefore inevitable operation of the "iron law of wages."

Long hours of toil, even as they could tend a machine or sweep a chimney, became the common lot. As a result, by far the most of the individuals in England's "lower classes" lived in squalor, compared with which the beasts of burden were well off; at least, the latter were valuable property, the health and condition of which was a matter of concern to their owners.

Naturally, many Englishmen were revolted by the conditions that accompanied material progress. Such men questioned the worth of progress at that price and in the end, to analyze conditions they deplored, sought drastic means of alleviating the conditions of the poor. Consequently, socialism in England found many of its intellectual leaders among such warm-hearted citizens and its voting strength in the great army of the underprivileged.

Fortunately for the United States, conditions here were more propitious. The availability of a vast extent of free or nearly free land for many decades postponed the more devastating effects of partial freedom. But there was special privilege here also, special privilege such as that enjoyed by the owners of great landed estates in England as well as other forms of special privilege.

Interference with and consequent distortion of free-market relationships result in special privileges that have become important here in the United States. These interferences and distortions of free-market relationships include (1) Government policies such as the price-support program, (2) trade associations or similar pressure groups that establish monopoly prices, and (3) inflation. Whenever the exchange relationships are such that prices are continually changing not only as a result of economic supply and demand but also because of the demand made possible by inflationary purchasing media, astute speculators are given an artificial advantage that they would not ordinarily enjoy.

Another major cause of an inequitable distribution of currently produced wealth has been the granting of special privileges in the form of rights to exploit natural resources, rights given to some segments of the society at the expense of others.

The effects of disinheriting a substantial portion of a nation's citizens, of denying to them equal opportunities to use natural resources, have been clearly seen in other countries by many men. For example, the Bell Report on the Philippines discussed the necessity of permitting Philippine peasants to break the stranglehold of the landlords and retain the fruits of their labor. Dr. Bunche, acting on behalf of the United Nations, intended to institute such reforms in Korea but apparently was rebuffed by the authorities placed in charge. Land reform of this nature is well underway in Japan. Italy has initiated such reforms. Secretary Brannan has stated that the key to Asia's poverty is land reforms, Supreme Court Justice Douglas has proposed the same solution for the problem of extreme poverty in Asia, and recent articles in *Fortune* and *The New York Times Magazine Section* stress the need for a redistribution of land holdings in Asia.

Many observers who see the problem clearly in Asia and in other areas are unaware that the same problem exists to a degree here in the United States. The situation has been less acute here, apparently because the near approach to individual freedom for many decades has so raised the level of material well-being that only in times of severe depression has the plight of a large portion of the underprivileged become desperate.

Other monopolies such as those found in some industries and in some labor unions, insofar as they constitute special privileges that enable the individuals concerned to take unearned wealth at the expense of their fellow men, lessen individual freedom in the United States.[10]

The Counterrevolution

Not only in England and in the growing slums of the United States were the evil effects freedom seen. In much of Europe, conditions far worse than those developing in the United States and even worse than those found in England were the lot of the common people. Consequently, the revolt against freedom found supporters throughout Western Civilization. Karl Marx and his followers on the continent of Europe and the Fabian Society in England became the leaders of the counterrevolution.

Like many other idealists, however, the early Socialists including their militant group, the Communists, were more quick to discern evils than to analyze the underlying causes of the conditions they deplored. Consequently, it is not surprising that they chose what seemed to be the simple and obvious way to correct the inequitable distribution of wealth. Instead of seeking the elimination of special privilege and toward freedom (as described here), they urged that the state intervene directly in order to force a different distribution of currently produced wealth. "From each according to his abilities, to each according to his means" was a principal slogan of the counterrevolutionists.

Because they believed that the Great Revolution had brought to men more evil than good, the Socialists urged a retreat from the troubles of partial freedom in the arms of an all-powerful state. However, the state that they wanted to create was to be different from the states that some of mankind had overthrown in the struggle for individual freedom. The Socialist state was to be a beneficent despot rather than a capricious tyrant, a would create for its citizens the Utopia of which men had dreamed.

However, the Socialists overlooked those principles of economics, those patterns of economic behavior that seem like the "natural laws" of physics in their inevitable operation; and the Socialists paid too little heed

---

10 For a more comprehensive discussion of this subject, particularly as applied to conditions in the United States, readers are referred to an article by E.C. Harwood. "The Full Significance of Freedom," *The American Journal of Economics and Sociology*, January 1945, p. 191.

to the bitterly learned lesson, "Power corrupts, and absolute power corrupts absolutely." Conditions in England are the logical result of socialism at the part-way point; and the Union of Soviet Socialist Republics is the end result of socialism.

Space does not permit discussion in detail of the extent to which the counterrevolution has "succeeded" in the United States. In spite of the gains attributable to the great degree of freedom here, there are many Americans who no longer have confidence in freedom; they may pay it lip service, but their actions belie their words. A striking example is provided by the headlong rush to place the economy in a straitjacket of bureaucratic controls as the first step in preparing to preserve our freedom (the controls established during the Korean War).

Thus the counterrevolution gains momentum within Western Civilization aided by many men seeking to remedy the evil effects of partial freedom. Unaware that the evils they would correct are to freedom itself, they no longer trust liberty, and they fail to realize that the reactionary policies they espouse must carry Western Civilization back to the Dark Ages that preceded the Great Revolution.

Individual Freedom and Land Reforms

THE ELIMINATION of special privileges, especially those related to monopolies of land (sites and natural resources), is an effective means of combating the counterrevolution. Fortunately, Denmark and New Zealand provide excellent examples of the application of the basic principles of land reform. Within these two countries we may trace the development away from land-holding systems that once made men virtually slaves of the landlords to land-holding systems that have restored a large degree of individual freedom.

Denmark

Serfdom in Denmark was abolished by the edict of King Christian V in 1702. The effects of the edict, however, were temporary; and by 1733, under the provisions of the *Stavnsbaand*, peasants from 14 to 36 years of age were formally bound as villeins to the estates on which they were born. Although *Stavnsbaand* was not ended officially until 1788, Queen Magdalene in 1761 took the first major step toward genuine land reforms by making the peasants on her personal estates essentially freeholders. Her example quickly was followed by the prominent landowner, A. P. Bernstorff: and soon many other landowners had joined the movement.

An ordinance in 1771 specifically limited the kinds and amounts of compulsory service to be rendered by tenants. Later, the policies of Crown

Prince Frederick, who had achieved power in 1784 by a coup d'etat, were influenced greatly by the Danish landowner Reventlow. Apparently on the advice of the latter, peasants were exempted from most of their former obligatory services, land was allotted to them, buildings were moved for them, and many farmers were made owners or freeholders.

Under the guidance of Count Reventlow, an agricultural commission was appointed to investigate the condition of the entire peasant class and to examine specifically the question of land tenure. Important reforms resulted. In 1787 the landlords were deprived of judicial authority over their tenants. Finally, in 1800 the merging of peasant farms with larger properties was forbidden.

In the period from 1800 through 1849 the gains made during the earlier period were consolidated, and further reforms were initiated. In Denmark, as in the rest of Europe at this time, the power of the absolute monarchy was being challenged. In 1819 the absolute monarchy was abolished and the "free constitution," which provided universal manhood suffrage, was established.

Land-reform legislation of the new government continued through the quarter of a century from 1850 to 1875. Acts passed in 1850 reduced the exemptions from ground-rent taxes and abolished the service obligations still remaining on some farms and houses. Monrad's Law of 1861 was responsible for promoting the change from leasehold tenancies to freehold land. Improvement of leases and sales was promoted further by the Act of 1872. By the end of this period, more than 75 percent of Danish farms had become freehold.

Land reforms since 1875 have two principal types. One has been concerned with making loans more readily available to associations that promote small holdings of land and to small owners directly. The second type has been concerned with taxation.

In 1895 an act authorized state loans to applicants who fulfilled the conditions for becoming state cotters. In 1906 an act permitted state loans to societies or associations that would buy large properties for allotment purposes. Since 1899 the state has aided in establishing two-thirds of the more than 30,000 new small holdings.

A national land-value tax on all land (urban and rural alike) was instituted by the Act of 1922. The Act of 1926 provided that local taxes be calculated at one rate on the land value of every property, accompanied by another and lower rate on the value of improvements. Moreover, taxes on improvements were lowered further by exempting a specified amount from taxation. In 1933 the greater part of county taxation, which is levied only on real estate, was transferred to the value of land apart from improvements.

Tithes were abolished in 1903, and entail and feoffment were abolished in 1919. Finally, in 1925, legislation was passed that required all farms to be permanently maintained as independent properties.

The development of free access to the land in Denmark has evolved through three major stages. The first occurred early in the modern history of the country when the monarchs and many noblemen landowners enabled the great bulk of the peasants to become freeholders. The second stage, which occurred after the fall of the absolute monarchy, was characterized by a conscious effort of the government (through reform legislation and state loans) to create an greater subdivision of large estates and to establish a nation dominated by small landholdings. The third stage, that of a modified land-value taxation, has occurred in the last three decades. The effects of stage may be observed more clearly in New Zealand, where taxation has played a more significant role.

New Zealand

Discovered in 1642 by Tasman, what is now New Zealand was not explored to any great extent until Cook visited the islands in 1767. The first English missionaries did not land until 1814. Nevertheless, by the 1870's, much of the land was concentrated in large holdings.

In the general land regulations of 1853, the Waste Lands Act of 1854, and the Compact of 1856 the Crown recognized the waste lands as a function of the provincial councils. In order "to encourage immigrants to settle down, the provinces threw large areas of land on the market. Thousands who had been encouraged to come to the country in the hope of obtaining land found themselves utterly unable to compete with the wealthy classes.

The market was closed absolutely to the genuine small settler, and there was a rapid aggregation of land in the hands of the few."[11]

Some settlements of small holdings were made, especially in the North Island; but, in general, ownership of the land became concentrated in large holdings.

The demand for land reforms increased from 1876 until the election of 1890 although there was little abatement of land accumulation. In 1876 provincial system was swept aside.

In 1878 the ministry of Sir George Grey, whose early adult experiences in Ireland apparently had made him the convinced and bitter enemy of large landowners, introduced a land tax that was intended to break up the many large estates. Before the effectiveness of the land tax could be estimated, the speculative of land boom the 70's broke. In the depression that followed, the land tax was repealed (1879), and a property tax was substituted.

By 1890 about 80 percent of the people had no land, and slightly more than 1 percent of the landowners held 40 percent of the land values.[12]

In the elections of that year, the slogan "Back to the Land" had gained overwhelming support. According to Mr. Scholefield the Government came into being in 1891 as the result of the organized opinion of men who wanted land.

Two major types of reforms were initiated, those founded on taxation and those based on state purchase of land by agreement or compulsion. Between 1889 and 1907 the acreage of individual holdings of more than 10,000 acres was reduced by nearly 3,000,000 acres. Mr. Parsons has asserted, "Government purchases were largely responsible, but 1-3 were the result of voluntary subdivision by owners to escape the graduated tax."

---

11 Guy H. Scholefield, *New Zealand in Evolution* (Charles Scribner's Sons, London, 1909), p. 163-164.

12 Frank Parsons, *The Story of New Zealand* (Philadelphia, Equity Series, 1904). Mr. Parsons and others warn of the unreliability of the contemporary data upon which these estimates and others are based. Nevertheless, the data are some indication of the general order of magnitude of the numerous large holdings. Other estimates are not far different from those of Mr. Parsons.

The basis of the tax program is the Land and Income Assessment Act of 1891 and the Rating on Unimproved Value Act of 1896. The former, which abolished the general property tax, included among others the following provisions:

(1) Improvements, livestock, personal property, small estates, and small incomes were exempted from taxation;

(2) A fixed percentage tax of 1 pence on the pound was levied on all remaining land values of not more than $25,000;

(3) A graduated tax was levied on land values above $25,000;

(4) A graduated tax on net incomes above the exemption value was levied;

(5) Special taxes as high as 20 percent were levied on absentee landowners and corporations.

The taxes were not so high that most large landowners chose to sell their land. Nevertheless, as taxes were increased during subsequent years, the pressure on large estates was substantial.

The Rating on Unimproved Value Act of 1896 enabled boroughs, counties, and independent towns, by popular vote, to adopt a tax system based on land value alone, excluding improvements. By 1948 nearly 60 percent of these local groupings had adopted the system. Because this type of tax is burdensome to owners of large land holdings, especially to those whose land is not being used, the trend toward smaller holdings has been especially rapid in some New Zealand cities.

The success of the government in purchasing the Cheviot estate in 1893 for subdividing into small holdings was widely heralded; and in 1894 the land minister was granted 500,000 pounds a year in order to purchase estates. A maximum acreage for estates was prescribed, the excess being subject to purchase by the Government at a value decided upon by mutual agreement or by the decision of a Compensation Court. Under this law closer settlement was pushed forward rapidly and energetically.

The further land reforms in New Zealand since the turn of the century have been primarily in the form of amendments to these early policies in order to make them more effective. In 1903 the graduated land tax was increased, and in the Land and Income Tax Assessment Act of 1907 the

graduated tax again was stiffened. In 1917 the non graduated tax on land
up to $25,000 was eliminated, and a single graduated tax was substituted.
The new tax was from 1 penny to sevenpence on a pound, including a
supertax of 50 percent and a further tax of 50 percent on the total amount
for absentee owners. In 1921-22 the maximum was raised to nearly 8 pence
on the pound, the super tax was lowered to 33.3 percent with a rebate of
10 percent of the whole tax as a reward for prompt payment. In 1923 the
super tax was lowered to 23.3 percent and in 1924 was eliminated entirely.

Meanwhile the program for providing land for all was extended.
In the Land for Settlement's Act of 1892 crown lands were leased for
999 years (described as a lease-in-perpetuity) at an unchanging rent of 4
percent on the prairie value. The Land Laws Amendment Act abolished
the lease-in-perpetuity and substituted renewable leases for 33 or 66 years
with the right of purchase at any time. By 1927 under this law nearly 8,000
persons had obtained tenure on more than 2,000,000 acres. The National
Endowment Act proclaimed 7,000,000 acres as an endowment in per-
petuity to be disposed of only on leasehold tenure. In 1920 the area was
increased to 9,000,000 acres and in 1930 was reduced to 6,750,000 acres.

Summary

Although Denmark and New Zealand provide striking examples of
progress toward the goals of the great revolution with respect to equality of opportunity to use natural resources, other developments in both
countries constituted partial retreats from freedom's goals in some aspects
of their economies. Various socialistic schemes have been adopted,
sometimes apparently in desperation as the needed land reforms gradually effected and sometimes apparently in an excess of zeal for legislative
reforms. The application of the principal of individual freedom of access
to the land in Denmark and New Zealand has discouraged the counterrevolution in those countries; but, to date at least, it has not prevented the
counterrevolution from succeeding to a marked extent.

Unfortunately, many leaders of the reform movements failed to
discriminate between methods such as the land reforms, which tended to

reduce special privileges and restore equality of opportunity, and socialistic methods of alleviating the plight of the underprivileged.

Consequently, some aspects of individual freedom have been lost to the increasing power of the state. Whether the people of these nations will ultimately cast aside socialistic devices and make further progress toward the goals of the Great Revolution remains to be seen.

Conclusions

Eliminating the special privilege that denies equality of opportunity to use or benefit from land and other natural resources is essential if Western Civilization is to survive. The basic appeal of communism is to the underprivileged of all lands; and, as long as special privileges for some are continued, there will be less than equality of opportunity and therefore a denial of freedom to others.

American Policy in the Short Run

THE STRUGGLE against the counterrevolutionary elements within Western Civilization cannot be won in the short run; winning that conflict is a long-run problem. Nevertheless, the struggle against communism can be lost in the short run if the Nation's foreign and domestic policy and its preparations for defense fail to cope with Russia's aims to dominate more territory.

Earlier we suggested the general nature of the long-term offensive action against the counterrevolution. However, such a long-term offensive of ideas to combat the Socialist ideology, of example by reorienting our own policies so that the United States will not continue to sponsor the counterrevolution at home, and of leadership in persuading the nations of the world to seek the goals of the great revolution, such an offensive will require several years to implement and many more years to reach its objectives. Thus the only offensive against the counterrevolution that can succeed will require time, and to gain that time should be a primary purpose of the Nation's short-term policies.

Readers may recall the warning we have already given that "our foreign policy during and immediately after World War II was a series of blunders precisely because we dealt with successive short-term situations as though there were no long-term fundamental conflict of aims or as though we were blind to other than immediate pressing developments. Such was our major error, and the lesson should not be forgotten."

Even before those words were published, the then Secretary of the Navy Matthews was advocating a preventive war; and, a few days later, General Anderson was suspended from the Air War College for expressing similar views. Such statements reveal virtually complete ignorance long-term problem involved. Even if we could destroy Russia's military power overnight, the long-term problem would remain unsolved.

Those who advocate a preventive war seem to reveal once again the truth of the maxim that power corrupts and absolute power corrupts absolutely. If American possession of the great power provided by nuclear weapons can have such an influence on the views of supposedly responsible men, we can only hope that less belligerent views will prevail until the citizens of the United States have an opportunity to think the long-term problem through and reorient American foreign and domestic policies.

Condemnation of a preventive war does not imply that the statements of Matthews and Anderson serve no useful purpose. Sentiment in favor of a preventive war apparently reflects a desire to substitute definite action for the hesitant, uncertain, and floundering foreign policy that this country has followed in recent years. We shall profit from these preventive war statements if we understand their psychological appeal and devise a foreign policy that the offensive, not the offensive of declared war, but an offensive of ideas, examples, and leadership; a foreign policy based on a definite program aimed at coping with the counter revolution.

Gaining Time

In order to gain the needed time, the Nation's short-run foreign policy must cope successfully with the immediate threat resulting from Russia's ambition for more territory and power. This phase of our short-term policy, therefore, is concerned primarily with adequate military preparation.

From a military point of view, containing Russia is largely a "defensive" action, "defensive" in that we must secure those land areas needed in order to prevent Russia from launching an effective attack on the United

States and those land areas that will permit the United States to launch effective counterattacks. (Land areas such as Korea, which is of little significance from a military standpoint, can serve this purpose only to a limited extent, if at all. Such areas apparently are important primarily as proving grounds for our means of coping with the long-run problem of the counterrevolution.)

In order to prevent a succession of "Koreas" in areas vital to the national defense, a declaration of policy backed by American armed forces or aided by American weapons and funds is essential. This declaration of policy should make clear to the world that we intend to keep Russia and her satellites out of specific areas by armed force and that, of course, we intend to continue our support of the Atlantic Pact.

The specific areas might be enough to encircle Russia, as would a line through Greenland, Iceland, Norway, Sweden, Germany, Italy, Greece, Turkey, Syria, Iraq, India, Burma, French Indochina, the Philippines, Formosa, and Japan; or they might simply constitute a protective shield in the east including Greenland, Iceland, England, France, Spain, and Africa and in the west another shield including the Philippines, Okinawa, and Japan. The final choice of the areas deemed essential to the national defense in the short run presumably would be made by the Joint Chiefs of Staff or a selected group of the Nation's military advisers.

Such a short-term program of "containing" Russia should not be confused with the problem of meeting an attack by the Soviet Union itself. The United States forces used to protect the areas selected should be in sufficient strength to overcome local Russian-inspired uprisings but should not be expected to wage a successful campaign against Russia itself. The specific areas chosen should be those essential to the short-term military security of the United States.

The adoption of a short-run policy such as that described, although defensive in its military aspects, would give the American people a definite program comparable in its psychological appeal to a "preventive war" or the declaration of war in Korea. The uncertainty regarding American action in the event of another Russian-inspired attack would be ended. Of course, we do not imply that such a policy should be forever unchanged;

it would have to be changed as circumstances changed, but the public should be kept informed. By adopting a definite policy subject to public debate and acceptance, the Nation can eliminate the waverings and the spur-of-moment decisions that have characterized American foreign policy in recent years.

Initiating the Offensive against the Counterrevolution

A second major objective of the Nation's short-term policies should be to make the public aware of the long-term problem and to encourage education of the public and debate of the issues involved. These are necessary steps preliminary to the long-term offensive of ideas, examples, and leadership intended to cope with the counterrevolution.

The significance of our short-term foreign and domestic policies in relation to the future of Western Civilization should become a matter of public knowledge and debate. A clear statement of the Nation's policies, free of the usual diplomatic generalities, should be formulated. The public should be informed that the only means of coping with the counterrevolution will take time and that our short-term policies should enable us to gain that time. A beginning might well be made as follows:

First, our foreign policy should be formulated after public debate and discussion.

Second, the widely prevailing confusion regarding American policy should be ended. General statements should be supplanted by unequivocal statements of our intentions.

Third, the apparent inconsistencies in American foreign policy in recent years should be explained if possible and in any event eliminated. We have aided Greece and Turkey, for a time we refused aid to Nationalist China, we fought a war in Korea, and we may or may not fight for Formosa. American citizens have a right and duty to understand what the objectives are.

Fourth, and perhaps most important, the public should be informed of actual commitments that have been made. There have been frequent references to the possibility that present difficulties are attributable in part to mistakes made at Yalta and after. The Yalta agreements apparently were only a few of the secret agreements made by either the President or high officials of the State Department. We believe that the time has come when all such secret agreements should be made public.

If the President believes that any such agreements should remain in effect, they should be drafted in the form of a treaty and submitted to the Senate for ratification as specifically provided in the Constitution. Then the public can pass judgement on them. Only after such procedure can the agreements become binding on the Nation for an extended period.[13]

Conclusion

If American foreign and domestic policies are to succeed in the short run, they must cope with the Soviet's ambitions for more territory and simultaneously encourage formulation of the policies that can cope with the long-term problems on the counterrevolution. By gaining the time needed to reorient our foreign and domestic policies, we shall have an opportunity to prepare for a successful offensive against communism.

---

13 Although not provided for by the Constitution, executive agreements may be necessary and have been accepted as legal as a temporary expedient, but there is some question as to how long such agreements may be valid. For example, many authorities on constitutional law concur in the view that executive agreements made by one President are not binding on his successor.

Economic Aspects of
National Defense

Introduction

SINCE THE END of World War II the United States has undertaken extensive projects in the interests of national defense. In accordance with the Truman Doctrine, military and civil aid to Greece and Turkey has been provided; in addition, the European Recovery Program, the Point 4 plan for aiding undeveloped countries, and the Atlantic Pact all have been offered as a means of strengthening the "national defense." In view of the economic costs involved, including that of our own military forces, an analysis of the economic aspects of our national defense is urgently needed.

The first question to be answered is, What is "national defense"? For the purposes of this series of articles, we shall use the phrase to refer to the means used to preserve our national identity and safety, means that provide protection against armed attack from without and against infiltration of subversive elements from within. Of course, as geographical distances have, in effect, been lessened by improved transportation facilities and as modern civilization has changed in other ways, the necessary means presumably have changed. Nevertheless, the definition suggested appears to be as valid today as it was in any other period of the Nation's history.

That the basic character of national defense has remained unchanged for many decades seems to have been forgotten by many who are concerned about present dangers. Much of this concern probably reflects the fears aroused by the alleged necessity for a "bipartisan" foreign policy, by the so-called "crises" that seem to be almost continuous, and by the "do something quickly" attitude of supposedly responsible statesmen.

The alleged necessity for a bipartisan foreign policy may be seriously misleading because it lends an aura of profound and exaggerated significance to the problem of national defense. The point of view seems to be a carry-over from wartime. We believe not only that a bipartisan policy is no longer necessary in order to save face or in order to present an appearance of unanimity but that it may do much harm. The need for "blind" cooperation has disappeared. What is needed now is intelligent, searching, and clarifying debate of the issues incidental to national defense.

The continuing succession of crises, actual and synthetic, also tends to inhibit rational consideration of the Nation's defense problems. Aided and abetted by the desire of the radio, newspapers, and movies to public's attention, "crises" after "crises" has been used by politicians seeking to influence public opinion. Our viewpoint is that the nature of the national defense problem is such that it cannot be solved by emotional reactions to the crisis technique: rational consideration of possible alternatives, a calm and collected weighing of pro's and con's is essential. If we do not not undertake such rational analysis in peacetime regardless of crises, real and synthetic, when shall we do it? The obvious answer is that logical analysis and debate should proceed.

All too frequently the solution proposed for a synthetic crisis is to do something quickly, without too much thought concerning the consequences. Doing nothing or pausing to reflect and to analyze before acting is rarely advocated by those who claim to know the right answer. Unfortunately, doing something that produces only a palliative effect has the disadvantage from the viewpoint of the public of leading to still another crisis. By doing something quickly, the Administration apparently is able to satisfy the public's desire for action, but such policies usually result in much waste of time, effort, and resources.

Our analysis of the economic aspects of national defense will deal with the problem objectively in the light of past history and the present situation, in the manner that we analyzed the European Recovery Program. The Constitution authorizes the use of the taxpayers' funds for the national defense. However, funds and the wealth they represent are scarce; they do not exist in such boundless quantities that they can be used for any project without foregoing alternative uses.

Unfortunately, the relative merits of the alternative uses of the funds concerned cannot be ascertained so precisely as might be wished. However, from one point of view, it is not so important that there be a precise determination of the relative merits of alternative uses; we contend only that an effort should be made to compare the relative merits of the alternative uses of the funds concerned. This is the economist's approach to the problem; we suggest that it is a common-sense approach also.

Threats to the National Defense

There is little reason to believe that the United States is threatened at this time by any nation or group of nations other than Russia or a Communist group of nations dominated by Russia. That a socialized England may eventually be a member of such a group is a possibility. However, this possibility appears to be so remote that we shall not consider it seriously. The Communists hope to destroy the capitalistic system and eventually control the world. Therefore, the United States, as the foremost capitalistic nation in the world, should not ignore the possibility of a Russian attack.

The nature of such an attack on the United States may assume any of the following forms: attack without invasion, actual invasion of the United States, or an infiltration or boring from within. Of course, any combination of the three types of attack is possible.

An attack on the United States without invasion presumably would involve bombing by plane or rockets of some sort. Just how far any other nation has developed the hydrogen bomb and rockets of corresponding destructive power is not known. However, even with the successful development of hydrogen bombs and rockets, ways and means of using them would have to be developed. Long-range bombers capable of withstanding fighter-plane assault and radar-controlled anti-aircraft would be necessary to make use of the hydrogen bomb. Possibly submarines capable of firing hydrogen rockets or launching planes large enough to drop hydrogen bombs might be used to make an effective attack on the United States. Regardless of the method used, however, no enemy nation can hope to destroy our facilities so effectively as to prevent reprisals and counteraction. This fear of counteraction apparently was responsible for the unwillingness of the Germans to use gas in World War II. Presumably a similar fear of reprisals would discourage an attack on the United States by bombing or rockets as long as we held the lead in the manufacture of hydrogen bombs.

Invasion of the United States would require a large and efficient air force, a substantial navy, and an especially large merchant marine, as well as the necessary ground troops. The difficulties of transporting troops and equipment and of maintaining supply lines would be enormous. Russia simply does not have the naval power and will be unable to manufacture the required auxiliary ships etc. for a long time to come.

On the other hand, the threat of an attack by infiltration and boring from within is greater. In this respect we face dangers from two elements: first, the infiltration of a Communist fifth column; second, the danger that a majority or a controlling minority of our own citizens will become Communists, knowingly or otherwise. In this connection, the increasing centralization of government in the United States increases the susceptibility of the Nation to usurpation by a coup d'etat. Moreover, failure to correct economic maladjustments may aggravate economic injustices, encourage the adoption of socialistic or communistic ideas, and so weaken the domestic, financial, and economic system of the Nation that a revolution could be easily affected.

Basis of Plans for
National Defense

FURTHER CLARIFICATION of our definition of national defense may be desirable. We are using the phrase to refer to the means used to preserve the national identity and safeguard its citizens and wealth, means that provide protection against armed attack from without and against infiltration or subversive elements within.

We believe that the current concern over the means of *preventing or avoiding* another war has tended to obscure the problem of national defense. *National defense is national in scope; it is concerned with maintaining the United States as a nation, not with establishing a nationless world or a community of nations free from strife.* As long as we intend to perpetuate the United States as a nation, as long as we desire to retain our national identity, we face the possibility of conflict. To be prepared to win that conflict is the problem of national defense.

A society based on the perpetuation of national identity faces an unavoidable struggle for a favorable balance of power. Therefore, if the United States desires to preserve its national identity, it is confronted with the problem of maintaining a favorable balance of power either alone (if it is powerful enough) or with other dominated or friendly nations. Unfortunately, a lasting peace among societies determined to perpetuate national identities never has occurred. No nation or society ever has maintained successfully a permanent balance of power in its favor.

Faced with these historic facts, the United States may adopt any one of several long-term goals including the following: (1) attempting to preserve the national identity as long as possible; (2) immediately giving up our national identity in order to establish a world community; or (3) retaining the national identity temporarily but at the same time progressing slowly toward a nationless world by giving up more and more of our national identity as the world becomes less and less nationalistically inclined.

Regardless of whether we adopt the first or third policy (the second policy seems to be impracticable at this time in view of the fact that few nations in the world apparently are ready to form a world community), the national defense involves protecting the United States from attack, either from without or from within. The national defense is not concerned with creating a favorable balance of power solely in order to discourage would-be aggressors; the national defense should not be confused with eliminating war or eliminating the possibility of an attack on the United States: the national defense is concerned primarily with the means for coping with attack sooner or later.

One important fact that should never be forgotten is that the potential enemy's actions are essentially unpredictable. That a course of action appears to be unreasonable from our point of view is no guarantee that the leaders in some other nation will have a similar viewpoint. For example, the Japanese apparently believed that the destruction at Pearl Harbor would so undermine and so completely destroy the effectiveness of our Navy as to make possible a final victory for Japan. At present, nuclear bombing of the United States by Russia may seem a remote possibility to us in view of our ability to counter attack, using the same means. Nevertheless, Russian leaders may be willing to gamble on the effects of our counteraction in order to deliver the first blow. In planning for the national defense, consideration should be given to every contingency no matter how improbable many persons believe any contingency to be.

In view of the weapons already developed as well as others that may be used in the future, the United States cannot expect to develop means of protection that will prevent an enemy attack from causing some destruction within our continental limits. The Maginot Line type of defense is even less likely to succeed in the future than it has in the past. More than ever before, the offense will be the best defense. Consequently, plans for national defense should include provision for the earliest possible and most effective attack on the enemy's vital and most vulnerable forces and installations.

National-defense plans should not ignore the time element. Should preparations be made to cope with an attack tomorrow, in 5 to 10 years, or at some indefinite time in the future? For example, we see no reason to prepare for any early Russian invasion of the United States. As we mentioned previously, Russia simply does not have the air force, navy, and merchant marine necessary for such an attempt.

Probably the only attack that need be feared in the near future (say within 3 to 5 years) is bombing from airplanes or by rockets from submarines. Any such attack would be imprudent as long as the United States holds the lead in the manufacture of nuclear bombs and rockets; nevertheless, Russian fear of reprisals could be slight. Sacrifices of human life apparently have been of little consequence to the present Russian leaders; therefore, those individuals, in order to gain an initial advantage or force us to acquiesce in their plans, might be willing to incur the risk that many thousands of Russian civilians might be killed by our counterattack. The possibility of such an attack on the United states should not be disregarded even in the immediate future.

After a few years such an attack on the United States may be more feasible than it may be at present. Presumably Russia will develop nuclear weapons similar to ours and the means of delivering them. Although land bases nearer than Russia's to the United States would be necessary now and in the near future for successful air bombing of our cities, that will no longer be the situation when Russia has large numbers of planes comparable to or better than the B-36 or long-range rockets.

At some indefinite future time, virtually unlimited bombing ranges and rockets that may be fired thousands of miles away may make possible an attack on the United States from any point within Russia.

Our national-defense plans, therefore, should include provisions for coping with an attack without an invasion in the near future and an attack with or without invasion after a few years. Moreover, although no serious threat of revolution seems to exist at present, overthrow of our Government by subversion should also be guarded against.

Importance of
Other Land Areas

UNTIL MEANS OF ATTACK have been developed that would make present distances between Russia and the United States insignificant, various land areas outside our continental limits will be important to the national defense for either or both of two major reasons. Denial of such areas to Russia would lessen the potential effectiveness of any attack on the United States, and use of these areas by our own forces would facilitate the counterattack that presumably would be our most effective national defense.

Land areas outside the United States may be militarily advantageous in many ways. Probably one of their main functions is to insure that the first major blows of a Russian offensive would be directed elsewhere than at the United States. Presumably either western Europe, parts of Africa and South or Central America, or Alaska would have to be occupied by the Russians before any major attack could be made on the United States. During a period when conquest of any of these areas was attempted, time would be available for the United States to mobilize its forces.

Denying the land areas indicated to Russia would limit the effectiveness of any military action against the United States. Without bombing bases outside of Russia, for example, the Soviet Union would be powerless at present to launch an extensive aerial attack against us; without naval bases outside of Russia an invasion of the United States would be virtually impossible; without control of the entrances to the Atlantic from the east attack by submarine launched rockets or bombs on our eastern seaboard would be difficult; and without suitable jumping-off places invasion by Russia would be impracticable.

One major function of land areas outside the United States would be to provide necessary waging aerial warfare against the enemy. For example, the bombing missions contemplated in the event of war against Russia would employ bases as far apart as Okinawa, Saudi Arabia, Alaska, Italy, Africa, and Great Britain. Although many of the flights could originate from or end at bases in the United States, the range even of the latest planes would prevent such planes from returning to an original base in this country. Consequently, the bases mentioned above are vital at present to the success of long-range bombing missions.

Somewhat the same problem is faced in naval warfare. Strategically located fueling stations, as well as supply depots, are necessary in order to maintain the effectiveness of our fleet. Naval bases nearer than the United States is to the entrances to the Atlantic Ocean from the east would be of great value in keeping the ocean shipping lanes free for the vast supplies that the merchant marine would be called upon to provide for forces located abroad.

Finally, in order to attack the Soviet Union, our ground forces would need jumping-off places (such as the British Isles and Japan) to those areas from which effective action could be taken against the Russian armies.

Apart from the direct military value to our armed forces of these land areas, still another aspect of the problem should be considered. To the extent that the United States is dependent on other countries for strategic war materials, those land areas may be vital to the national defense. However, much of the concern voiced over the scarcity of such materials as manganese is unwarranted. Because in recent years most of our supply of manganese has been obtained from Russia, statements have been made to the effect that the steel industry would have to reduce operations drastically within a matter of months if Russia stopped its shipments of manganese. As is the case with many similar "shortage scare" arguments, there is a tendency to think of conditions solely in relation to the status quo. This argument ignores the fact that large quantities of ore are imported from Russia not because Russia is the only source of supply but because Russia is the cheapest source of supply. During a war or long-term emergency, manganese not only could be obtained from Brazil, India, or Africa but could be produced from low-grade ores mined in the United States. Of course, the costs would be greater, but no unusual problems would be involved.

In our series of articles on the European Recovery Program[14] we presented the results of an exhaustive study of another important raw material and came to the conclusion that, "...although the oil in the Middle East may seem urgently desirable to the major oil companies involved, it is *not* of vital importance to the people of the United States." The United States is fortunate in that all of the raw materials essential to the national defense are available in this hemisphere. Therefore, no land areas elsewhere are vitally important as sources of essential materials.

The foregoing discussion of the value of other land areas will be applicable during the next few years. If the improvements in bombing planes make it possible for planes to leave bases in

Russia, effectively bomb strategic locations in the United States, and return to Russia without refueling, if rockets are developed that will be effective at distances of 4 to 5 thousand miles, if troops and supplies can be effectively transported over long distances by air, the importance to our national defense of land areas outside of the United States will be much less than it is today. Although these possibilities may appear to be remote, they warn us that any long-term national-defense program should not be based on the assumption that we shall always have the advantages derived from the availability to us of today's strategic land areas.

Foreign Policy

The scope of American foreign policy, insofar as it has been directed toward denying strategic areas to a potential enemy and assuring their availability for our use, has been increased far beyond the scope of the Monroe Doctrine in recent years. The so-called Truman Doctrine as it

---

14 *Where Are We Going?* By John J. Carter and E.C. Harwood.

seems to have been interpreted in fact,[15] the European Recovery Program, the at-present-somewhat-nebulous plan for undeveloped countries, and the Atlantic Pact are the principal means chosen to date.

Important as these means may be, certain general considerations pertaining to them should not be overlooked. In the first place, recent as well as more remote history amply demonstrates that treaties are not to be relied upon. We should not expect any treaty to be honored after it ceases to serve the best interests of either nation concerned.

Nor is the so-called friendship or good will between nations of value once a nation discovers that maintaining friendship or goodwill is in its own best interests. That rapid changes in the status of national affections can readily occur was seen not only in the prewar dealings between Hitler and Stalin but also in our own dealings with Russia.

Furthermore, gratitude for past favors or gifts should be given little weight. We cannot afford to forget that the decisions of other countries will be based on their estimate of their own *future* best interests. The fact that in the past the United States has been a beneficent friend should not be expected to influence any nation's choice between the United States and Russia. That decision presumably will be based on each country's estimate of its own future interests.

In a world of national states, any single nation must act with due regard to the balance of power if it is to survive as an independent nation. France, Germany, Belgium, or any other nation can ill afford to cast its lot with the weaker side of that balance. To do so is to risk losing the national identity. Consequently, rather than attempting to influence other nations by protestation of good will and by gifts, the United States should endeavor to maintain such a preponderance of industrial and military power that less powerful nations will jeopardize their security by failing to cooperate with us.

---

15 Interpreted broadly, the Truman Doctrine implied that the United States, in effect, would guarantee to the people of every nation of the world their choice of a form of government and protect it against invasion or domestic violence. (This guarantee would be similar to that given the 48 States of the Union under the Constitution.)

Clearly, favorable relations may best be achieved with other nations (especially those possessing or controlling land areas important to our national defense) by proving to those nations that it is to their own best interests to cooperate with the United States. As long as this proof is forthcoming, we have little reason to fear that desirable land areas will be denied to us.

Strength of Our Armed Forces

THE REMARKS of General "Jimmy" Doolittle prior to the Korean War remain especially pertinent to a discussion of the strength of our armed forces necessary for defense. "Our military establishment must be based on effectiveness, efficiency, and *economy*. It should be composed of the smallest Army, the smallest Navy, and the smallest Air Force which – properly organized and coordinated – will give us a reasonable degree of security. We cannot afford a combination War Department, maintained over an indefinite time, which will always be so prodigally manned and equipped as to permit us to win promptly any war into which we may be unfortunate to be plunged.... We could easily destroy ourselves through the dissipation of our resources in being always ready."

With the foregoing in mind, we shall endeavor to answer the question, How best can the Nation maintain the military strength, actual and potential, that will enable us to cope with surprise attacks, launch effective counterattacks, and ultimately defeat the enemy?

Certainly this strength will not be maintained by diverting troops and equipment to areas such as Korea that serve no useful purpose as part of our national defense.

Present Strength of Our Armed Forces

As of June 30, 1953, there were approximately 3,600,000 service men and women on active duty in the Armed Forces. Although estimates of Russian forces vary from 3,000,000 to 5,000,000 men, we see no need of maintaining large ground forces in the United States. The threat of invasion in the near future is negligible; consequently, our defense does not require a large standing army.

Moreover, although a Russian submarine attack might be undertaken, the Russians are unable to provide adequate naval support for an invasion of the United States. Consequently, at present there does not seem to be any need for maintaining a vast navy for defense against such action. On the other hand, the threat of Russia's submarines justifies maintenance of naval forces capable of protecting at least some of the shipping lanes to our forces and allies in Europe and elsewhere.

Comparative data of United States and Russian air power are scarce. We do not know exactly how many modern planes the U.S.S.R. does possess. Nevertheless, until the Russians can produce long-range bombers that compare favorably with our own on the scale that our industry can produce such planes, there is little reason to fear a sustained air attack on the United States.

A more extensive discussion of our present strength does not seem pertinent. We have indicated that our national-defense plans should include provisions for coping with an attack without invasion in the near future and an attack without or possibly with invasion after a few years. Plans for the near future depend do not depend so much on the quantitative strength

of our armed forces as on the development system and strategic and specialized air and naval defensive units.

Necessary Strength of Armed Forces to Meet Threat
After a Few Years

Attempts to calculate how many troops will be necessary after the next 5 or 10 years, how many planes we shall need, or how many naval ships will make possible effective control of the high seas probably would be frustrated by unforeseen developments. Changes in the methods of warfare brought about by new scientific developments could quickly outmode any plans made at present. More important, we do not possess the wealth necessary in order to remain in complete readiness for war at all times. Therefore, the military strength needed to meet the threat of an attack with or without invasion after a few years must depend primarily on the following: the efficient organization and training of the armed forces including reserves, the adequacy of our warning systems, the continuous development of new and more effective weapons, our means for launching rapid and effective counteraction, and our ability to convert rapidly to production of the items needed for the war of the future.

Efficient Organization

One of the primary requisites of a strong military establishment is the development of a sound Department of Defense. The findings and recommendations of the Hoover Commission on The National Security Organization were based on the belief that… "the most careful possible utilization of our energies and resources must govern every operation of the National Military Establishment."

The Committee, however, failed to find in the Military Establishment a sense of cost consciousness or a general realization of the vital importance to our national security of utmost conservation of our resources. Extravagance, waste, and duplication must be removed in order to create efficient organization.

Although the Unification Act eliminated some of the inadequacies of our present military organization, others mentioned by the Commission still exist.

Training of Armed Forces and Reserves

To a far greater extent than many people realize, the rapid progress of American industry in the past reflected the early successes of relatively young men. Several of the American corporations that are leading the technological advance today were begun by young men. The early maturing of their organizing and technical genius enabled them to build industrial empires that added greatly to the Nation's productive power. Hundreds of less widely known industrial concerns likewise owe their existence to the energy, inventiveness, characteristic of American youth in its best years.

The time taken from men's lives in order to train them to be soldiers therefore should be the minimum consistent with achieving the desired results. We can ill afford to postpone by years the scientific education and technical training of the Nation's youth. Industry even now cannot find a number of graduate engineers sufficient to meet its needs; the number of doctors becoming available at present also presumably is inadequate; and the competently trained social scientist is a rarity. If the situation is so grave today, how much graver that situation will be as a result of shutting off the flow of replacements entirely for 2 or 3 years. Moreover, because of the lack of a program, many boys (who would otherwise be making plans for the future and taking steps to implement those plans) are reluctant to undertake a career that may be interrupted at any moment and therefore are contributing little, if anything, to the Nation's welfare. How, then, can *adequate* military training of American young men be compressed into the shortest practicable time?

Good soldiers can be trained in a few months; moreover, even years of training will not necessarily produce good soldiers. Much depends on the training given. Excellent officers can be trained from college graduates in less than 5 months. As for the non-commissioned officers and privates who necessarily constitute about nine-tenths of any army, wholly untrained young men can be trained to a high order of discipline, soldierly smartness, and ability to care for themselves in the field in 6 weeks.[16]

One fact that should not be forgotten is that an army of several million men cannot be transported overseas to a fighting front in less than several

---

16 In congressional hearings relevant to lowering the draft age, queries as to the quality of replacements for service in Korea were answered by an Army representative by pointing out that the troops were not recruits but men who had received 15 weeks of training and were thoroughly prepared for combat service.

months. While waiting for their turn to go, the less well-trained units would have ample time for intensive field training.

The following outline of a training program is suggested as a means of giving American youth the training required without greatly postponing the scientific and technical training of those who will be needed to insure the maximum development of American industry:

On June 1 of the year in which each young man graduates from high school or on June 1 following his eighteenth birthday, whichever comes earlier, each physically fit young man who had not volunteered for one of the armed services should be required to undertake during the summer months intensive training in the field *directly under the supervision* of and as a member of greatly expanded Regular Army units.[17]

Every physically fit young man who was privileged to receive a college education would be required to participate in the ROTC (or similar naval or air force units). Additional noncommissioned officers would be provided by requiring ROTC students to come to a summer training period as acting noncommissioned officers after their freshman or sophomore years. Additional officers (provisional second lieutenants) for the increased number of units would be drawn from ROTC students in the summer after the junior year (the normal summer-camp period), from Reserve officers newly commissioned on graduation from college who would be required to serve 4 months on active duty, and from other Reserve officers called to active duty for a month at a time.

Men for the Regular Army would be obtained by voluntary recruiting as is done now and by drafting such trainees, by lot, as were needed.

Although the foregoing is hardly more than a general outline and would be subject to modification as experience indicated better procedures, it is definite enough to make clear that certain great advantages would result. Instead of taking 2 or more years from the life of every young man as has been proposed and postponing his industrial training and scientific education accordingly, those who did not go to college would be

---

17 The Army's construction program of $2,400,000,000 suggests an investment in facilities that hardly would be warranted by other than a permanent "force in being" ready to fight a major war, certainly not by the needs of a group undergoing intensive *field* training.

delayed only 4 months in their industrial training and would be required to serve only 1 or 2 months more in later years, and those who went to college would be delayed only 4 months after graduation in pursuing their normal careers. The man-hours lost to industry, science, and the technological advance would be but a fourth or a fifth of the loss under a 2-year or 27-month training program.

Early Warnings and
New Weapons

OUR ARMED FORCES should have the earliest possible warning of an impending attack on the United States. The warning, in order to be used most advantageously, should come during the planning stages of any such attack. Consequently, a well-organized intelligence system is essential. Of course, we cannot put our complete faith in espionage. A practical mechanical warning system also must be in continuous operation.

The Hoover Commission seriously criticized the Nation's intelligence operations. "Intelligence is the of defense in the atomic age. Recognition of its preeminent role in defense planning was given in the National Security Act by creation of the Central Intelligence Agency..." The relationships of this agency to some of the other intelligence agencies of Government – notably to G-2 of the Army, the Federal Bureau of Investigation, the Atomic Energy Commission, and the State Department have been and still are unsatisfactory.

"The Central Intelligence Agency is sound in principal, but improvement is needed in practice. It is not now properly organized. A serious deficiency is the lack of an adequate top-level evaluation board or section, whose duties are confined solely to the evaluation of intelligence, with no responsibilities for general policy or administrative matters.

Even a well-organized, efficient, and competent intelligence, however, must be supplemented by mechanical means of detecting attack from

the sea or air. The Navy, the Coast Guard, and the Air Force must maintain anti submarine detectors, radar, and radio-wave identification and
adequately patrol the sea lanes and the airways by naval units and planes.

Development of New Weapons

Ex-President Truman's disclosure of an atomic explosion in Russia
was a dramatic reminder that, in spite of American industrial progress, the
scientific advance is not confined to the United States.[18]

During World War II we saw ample evidence of the engineering and
scientific skill of the scientists of other nations: radar was first developed
and used most effectively by the British; rockers were first developed and
used most effectively by the Germans; and Russian tanks were admittedly
superior to the American Grants and Shermans.

On the other hand, numerous developments, including the atomic
bomb, radio-controlled shells, and the world's largest heavy bombers,
were primarily the achievement of American scientists and American mass
production. Fortunately, there is little question that, on the whole, scientific progress in the United States is far ahead of that in Russia.

To maintain our lead over Russia in the development of modern
weapons is vitally important, but, unfortunately, our progress in that
respect is not so satisfactory as it might be. Of the more than a billion dollars spent by the Federal Government on scientific research and development, more than $600,000,000 is disbursed by the military departments.
According to the Hoover Commission, "under present conditions the
country is not getting full value from these expenditures. A satisfactorily
'complete and integrated program of research and development for military purposes,' does not exist."

---

18 We see no reason for added concern over the disclosure that Russia has created an atomic
explosion. The atom bomb at present is one of the most effective destructive weapons developed by man. However, even if Russia has the bomb, it will not be effective as a weapon against
us until large numbers can be transported to targets here; furthermore, the atom bomb is not so
effective that its use would insure immediate or even ultimate victory; finally, there is no assurance that even the atom bomb will not be outmoded within several years.

If we are to have adequate military strength, we cannot afford to ignore the necessity of a continuing search for new and more effective weapons. Push-button bombing, the harnessing of solar energy, so-called "germ warfare," and other seemingly remote and far-distant weapons of total war must be studied, worked on, and developed to the point where, to the extent practicable, they become part of our arsenal of weapons.

If we are to avoid excessive costs, however, this continuing search should take advantage of all that is daily in the Nation's industry. Our most formidable weapons during World War II were made possible by research that had been undertaken during peacetime in order to improve industrial processes and develop new commercial products. There is much truth in the assertion that tomorrow's military weapons will, indirectly, be developed from today's television sets and electric dishwashers.

Means of Counteraction

The ability of the Nation's armed forces to initiate rapid and effective counteraction following any attack on the United States or areas vital to its safety is believed to be urgently desirable, perhaps essential, in order to win the war. Even an attack not accompanied by actual invasion of the continental United States or other areas we choose to defend should be countered as rapidly and is practicable. Such counterattacks would be the best means of hampering the enemy's armed forces and lessening his war potential while our military and industrial power were being mobilized for the ultimate and decisive tests on world battlegrounds.

An enemy attack without invasion presumably would be from the air, although an attack might be launched from submarines. Our counterattack, therefore, must be directed against the enemy's submarines, aircraft, and bases.

An efficient counterattack force capable of almost immediate action, intelligence services, and other means (such as the radar net) that can provide a timely warning, and an adequate stock pile of atomic bombs or other weapons to be used by the counterattack force are essential. In addition to the discussions of these matters already presented, other considerations should be mentioned.

Preparation for immediate counteraction presumably would involve a minimum of ground forces. General Devers, former Chief, Army Field Forces, stated before his recent retirement that he expected to have 6 months in which to prepare for offensive ground action even if a war came suddenly. During that period substantial ground forces could be mobilized, and in the meantime our counterattacks presumably would be entirely by air and sea.

Another possibility, improbable now but more probable after a potential enemy has accumulated the required means, would be an attack involving actual invasion of the United States. Ground forces in sufficient numbers to aid air and naval action in preventing the invasion would be necessary. However, the enemy troops that could be brought in by air or sea in the foreseeable future would be so few in number that they presumably could be disposed of by a relatively small United States ground force.

In either situation, therefore, preparations for rapid and effective counteraction must be based primarily on an air force capable of striking back hard at the enemy while the navy controls the sea. Emphasis in preparing for a counterattack should be on creating an air force and a navy that can delay the enemy and reduce his effectiveness while are being prepared for a major offensive.

We should remember that the purpose of the initial counterattack will not be to conduct the major offensive. Consequently there is no need to maintain large armed forces on a fully mobilized basis.

Conclusion

Because actual invasion in the next few years apparently is not threatened, a large standing army and an air force and navy at full fighting strength would involve an uneconomical use of available resources including manpower. Even from the viewpoint of national defense alone, we are convinced that men and materials used in the normal course of industrial progress and production will contribute more in the long run to the national defense than would use of the same men and materials for the maintenance of a large standing army, air force, and navy. The magnitude of our armed forces maintained in a state of readiness should be the minimum compatible with our primary national-defense needs; that is, sufficient for effective counteraction against an attack without an invasion in the near future and an attack with or without an invasion subsequently, and sufficient to serve as the nucleus of the forces to be mobilized when war threatens.

Industrial Capacity and National Defense

THAT A NATION'S industrial capacity is of great importance in modern warfare became increasingly clear during the last two world conflicts. Of course, manpower is essential in order that a nation's output may be used successfully; and the relative mental health and physical characteristics of one nation's citizens compared with those of another country should not be overlooked. However, we believe that, in a war between the United States and Russia, comparative manpower is and for some time to come will continue to be a relatively unimportant factor. Comparative industrial potential probably will be the decisive factor in any war in the foreseeable future.

Military Importance of Peacetime Industry

Many of a nation's war needs are precisely or nearly the same as those of peacetime. The kinds of food, clothing, shelter, and transportation used by the armed forces are essentially unchanged from the corresponding peacetime products.

A nation's remaining war needs require in most instances the basic factors of production developed in peacetime. Raw materials such as coal, iron, oil, copper, and raw steel are suitable for either peacetime or wartime use. Similarly, in peacetime, workers generally develop skills equally applicable to wartime production. Research facilities, laboratories, and testing grounds are immediately available to the wartime industrial machine. Finally, most of the plant and much of the industrial equipment are immediately usable for or soon can be adapted to military production.

Therefore, the production of the implements of war is not something apart from and unrelated to a nation's peacetime industrial plant and equipment. On the contrary, output of war materials is achieved largely by using the existing productive capacity, either directly or to some extent indirectly by utilizing it to provide additional specialized facilities. What, then, is the relative standing of the United States with respect to industrial potential?

Developments to Date

Comparisons of industrial production in the United States, Russia, Great Britain, France, and Germany reveal that, since 1890, industrial production in the United States has exceeded that of any of the other nations.[19]

The most striking development revealed by these comparisons was an extremely high rate of gain for Russia from 1923 to 1939. However, such gains were to be expected as a result of the application of industrial techniques, already developed elsewhere, in a country such as Russia, where industrial development had been seriously retarded.[20]

Russian capacity to produce increased rapidly during those years primarily for two reasons: (1) modern machine tools and engineering knowledge were obtained from the leading industrial nations; and (2) the numbers of additional workers drawn into industry were large in relation to the numbers so employed when the transition began. There is still no indication that Russia has developed superior ability to invent and apply new industrial techniques.

---

19 Data compiled from several sources were linked together in order to provide a rough estimate of the general orders of magnitude involved. Russian figures for recent years were based on the production records for specific commodities indicated in the table presented later.

20 Maurice Dobb, *Soviet Economic Development Since 1917* (International Publishers, New York, 1943) and S.S. Balzak et al., *Economic Geography of the USSR* (Macmillan, New York, 1949.)

Comparative increases in productivity per worker in the United States and Russia reflect a development similar to that which occurred in production.[21]

From 1920 to 1940 Russian productivity (including agriculture) increased 1.8 times. Productivity in the United States during the same period increased only 1.6 times. However, productivity in the United States was 6.2 times that of Russia in 1920 and 5.6 times in 1940. In other words, although the rate of increase of Russian productivity was greater than that of the United States for two decades, Russian productivity was so low in 1920 that by 1940 the productivity of American workers was still nearly 6 times as great as that of Russian workers.

After World War II, production in the United States recovered much more rapidly than did that of any other major country including Russia. Consequently, the difference by which American output has exceeded Russian output has substantially increased since 1938.

Present Situation

In spite of the rapid development Russian economy, Soviet industry is still substantially undeveloped in comparison with that of the United States. The data in the accompanying table reveal that, with the exception of coal production, which was curtailed markedly during 1950 because of strikes, United States output of each product is more than 2.5 times that of Russia. Especially important are the differences in steel, petroleum, and electric-power production. Moreover, the ability of the United States to produce more than 20 automotive vehicles for every one that

---

21 This discussion is based on a study of productivity rates made by Colin Clark, Australian government economist. The data are to appear in a new edition of the Macmillan publication *The Conditions of Economic Progress*. In commenting on the data in an article in the August 21, 1949, edition of *The New York Times*, Mr. Will Lissner said, "His [Clark's] former estimates have been criticized on several grounds..." Since that time however, his estimate of the Soviet national income for 1939 has been confirmed by independent estimates made on the basis of wholly different approaches..." Readers are reminded that estimates of productivity are difficult to make and are subject to many qualifications. Our own estimates of industrial productivity in the United States (excluding agriculture) are similar to Mr. Clark's from 1920 to 1940. During the war and afterward, however, our estimates are substantially below those offered by Mr. Clark.

Output of Selected Industrial Products
In The United States and Russia

| | 1937 | | | 1950 | | |
	Russia	U.S.	Ratio U.S.:Russia	Russia*	U.S.	Ratio U.S.:Russia
Steel (millions of tons)	19.3	56.6	2.9	26.5	97.0	3.7
Coal (millions of tons)	139.1	497.4	3.6	288.0	555.3	1.9
Petroleum (millions of barrels)	193.2	1,279.2	6.6	265.8	1,973.0	7.4
Electric Power (billions of kw hours)	36.4	118.9	3.3	90.5	378.3	4.2
Pig Iron (millions of tons)	16.0	41.5	2.6	19.5	65.0	3.3
Tractors (thousands)	32.2	272.4[§]	8.5	180.0	520.0[§]	2.9
Automotive Vehicles (millions)	0.1*	4.8	48.0	0.4	8.0	20.0

§ Does not include tractors for non-farm use; *Estimated

Russia produces seems significant when one remembers the increased importance of mechanization in warfare.

Not only is American production of potential war material greater than that of Russia; but also, and perhaps of even greater significance, American productivity per worker as late as 1947 was 8.5 times that of Russia (based on Mr. Clark's estimates).

Soviet inefficiency since the war has been attributed to many factors including the following: (1) reconversion has been hindered by a cumbersome bureaucracy; (2) there has been a lack of skilled workers, much of the labor force being relatively new to industrial production; (3) machines have been in poor condition because of hard use and inadequate maintenance during the war; (4) labor discipline has been poor, and the labor turnover has been high; (5) there has been much waste and unproductive expenditure; and (6) managerial efficiency has been poor.

Near-Future Possibilities

If Russia could regain her prewar rate of industrial progress, Soviet production would exceed that of the United States in some important respects within a few years. However, aided by tools and technology borrowed from more advanced industrial societies, the rapid stage of industrial development has already occurred. Presumably a similar opportunity to borrow progress will not occur again unless Russian industrial development lags far behind that of other nations. Consequently, there is little reason to believe that Russia's industrial capacity will compare favorably with that of the United States in the near future.

Another important obstacle tending to prevent resumption of Russia's prewar rate of progress is the fact that fewer relatively idle factors of production (land, labor, and capital) are available in industry. We have already indicated that increased output of goods in Russia has resulted from the use of increased physical quantities of the productive factors rather than from increased efficiency of management and greater productivity per worker. Apparently, future gains must come largely from gains in efficiency, an aspect of industrial progress that bureaucratic regimes seem to hinder rather than to foster.

But, some persons ask, what if the United States should have a major depression within the next few years. Fear of a depression "bogey man" seems to be influenced more by emotion than by even a hasty consideration of the facts. Our long-term economic growth has occurred in spite of recurring depressions. Moreover, a depression would not destroy the Nation's industrial potential. No great decrease in the available plant and equipment would occur, nor would the available labor force be depleted to any great extent.

The More Distant Future

In attempting to estimate the relative industrial potential of the United States and the Soviet Union in the more distant future, the following two important aspects of the problem should be considered: (1) the potential quantity of the basic factors of production that are available to each country and (2) the relative rates of growth to be expected in the two countries.

The quantity of land and labor[22] available to Russia as now constituted is far that available to the United States. What, then, is the possibility that Russian industrial production will exceed that of the United States in the long run?

In order to answer the foregoing question, we must appraise the economic systems within which the necessary progress is to occur. As we have already indicated, the progress Russia has made in the past three decades is attributable not to the economic advantages of communism but to the transition from an agricultural to an industrial nation.[23]

The real test of efficiency of Russia's planned economy has not yet occured.

We do know that the transition, rapid as it has been, has been hampered by the inefficiencies of bureaucracy. We do know that the production of the Soviet has been overstated because of the relatively inferior quality of much of the output. We do know that progress has not been uniform, that some industries have progressed too rapidly, other industries too slowly. We do know that part of the annual production feats has been at the expense of allowing the country's plant and equipment to deteriorate.

How much of any specific failing can be attributed directly to the communist form of economy is difficult to ascertain. Nevertheless, we believe that a system that denies man his freedom cannot hope to compete with a system that guarantees far more freedom.

The effects of freedom of thought and speech are far reaching. Men are free to abandon unscientific explanations of events and seek the cause of known effects unhampered by the wishes of theologians, kings, or

---

22 Capital, which results from the application of labor to land and is essentially stored-up labor, the product of labor applied to land that is not immediately consumed, need not be considered at this point.

23 Of course, the transition was forced by a communist government employing communistic techniques. However, there is no reason to believe the gains would have been less if the transition had been made under a democratic form of government; on the contrary, there is good reason to believe that the gains would have been much greater.

dictators. Under such circumstances, there is freedom for the application of the scientific method, which is our only tested means of obtaining the knowledge that provides the basis for technological progress. Finally, freedom of thought permits men to explore the unknown, while free speech permits the dissemination of the results of such explorations.

Liberty of action enables man to take advantage of new opportunities, to develop new uses for land, to seek new natural resources, and to initiate the development of wholly new industries.

Forcing economic activity into predetermined channels seems almost certain to retard economic progress. Thus far Russia has been able to take advantage of industrial techniques developed by other countries under other systems of government. As long as she retains communism, she probably will be forced to use methods developed for the most part in other countries, because Russia's scientific progress is somewhat retarded through the lack of freedom to follow paths not approved by the planners. As long as Russia must depend to a substantial extent on techniques developed in other countries, she cannot achieve a comparable stage of industrial development, she will always lag behind.

Dr. Vannevar Bush in his recent book *Modern Arms and Free Men* sums up the situation as follows: "Through the pattern of modern thinking runs a doubt, as to whether a system based on the dignity of man, built in good will, can be sufficiently strong to prevail. The thesis of this book is that such a system is far stronger, in dealing with the intricate maze of affairs that the applications of science have so greatly elaborated, than any dictatorship. The democratic system, in which the state is truly responsive to the will of the people, in which freedom and individuality are preserved, will prevail, in the long run, for it is not only the best system, the most worthy of allegiance that the mind of man has built; it is the strongest system in a harsh contest."[24]

The danger that faces the United States does not appear to be that Russia will achieve a rate of growth greater than ours is at present: the danger appears to be that our rate of growth will be reduced as a result of

---

24 Vannevar Bush, *Modern Arms and Free Men* (New York, Simon and Schuster, 1949), p.8.

our deviation from the path to freedom toward a socialist economy. The transition period, when neither the capitalistic nor the socialistic phases of the economy would be functioning most effectively, might drag on for a sufficient length of time to lessen seriously our industrial capacity. A communisistic economy might achieve greater industrial capacity than that of an economy floundering between capitalism and socialism. That the rate of growth in the United States since World War I has not been so great as that from the Civil War to 1914 may be attributable in part to the effects of increasing divergence from the equality of opportunity and economic freedom originally sought as the basis of our society.

Two Related Problems

Many observers have argued that a nation's industrial potential could be rendered almost impotent because its plant, equipment, and population would be vulnerable to ordinary bombing, guided missiles, or the atom or hydrogen bomb. However, such opinions seem to have been influenced more by emotions than by facts.

As for the atomic bomb (and we believe that his comments are equally applicable to the hydrogen bomb) Dr. Bush says: "The principal point is that the atomic bomb is for the immediate future a very important but by no means an absolute weapon, that is, one so overpowering as to make all other methods of waging war obsolete. It will remain in that status as long as there are not great stocks of bombs in the hands of more than one power, and even if this should occur it may remain in that category unless there also then exists means for delivery of the bombs onto enemy targets with at least a moderate degree of assurance... Those who argue that on the outbreak of war some time in the future all the principal cities of both belligerents will be promptly and utterly destroyed by mass fleets of bombers carrying atomic bombs... completely ignore the enormous strides being made in defense.[25]

There is no reason to believe that any war in the foreseeable future will be brought to a close so quickly that the industrial capacity of the

---

25 Ibid. p. 56

nations concerned will not be the deciding factor in determining the outcome.

A second popular notion is that a Russian economy geared for war (that is, concentrating on the production of essential war goods and materials), even though its over-all production were less than that of the United States, would be in a position to wage a successful war against us. Such a possibility seems remote. As we have already pointed out, the industrial facilities necessary for war are little different from those necessary for peace. Essential war materials such as steel, coal, oil, and power are equally essential for the production of consumer goods.

Conclusion

Russian industrial capacity has not been, is not at present, and in the near future will not be comparable to the industrial power of the United States. Furthermore, there appears to be no danger that Russia's industrial capacity will exceed or even approach that of the United States in the more distant future unless the progress of the United States is seriously retarded. Of course, if the United States continues in the direction of state planning and socialism, there is a serious possibility that, during the transitional period from capitalism to socialism, the Nation will be so weakened industrially that the Soviet Union would be in a position to attack effectively.

Choosing Wisely Among
Available Resources

ARLIER WE SAID that "as long as we intend to perpetuate the United States as a nation, as long as we desire to retain our national identity, we face the possibility of conflict. To be prepared to win that conflict is the problem of national defense."

Later we indicated our belief that "in a war between the United States and Russia, comparative manpower is and for some time to come will continue to be a relatively unimportant factor. Comparative industrial potential probably will be the decisive factor in any war in the foreseeable future."

And finally, we have concluded: "If the United States continues in the direction of state planning and socialism, there is a serious possibility that, during the transitional period from capitalism to socialism, the Nation will be so weakened industrially that the Soviet Union would be in a position to attack effectively."

The key, therefore, to the problem of national defense is primarily that of maintaining, or preferably increasing the difference of industrial potential that now exists between the United States and Russia. Other aspects of the problem, such as securing adequate air and sea bases, cultivating the friendship of other countries, or building vast air or sea armadas assume relatively minor importance when compared with the major job of maintaining the industrial superiority of the United States. Without that industrial superiority, not only will conflict with Russia become more probable but also America's chances of winning that conflict will diminish. How to preserve the industrial superiority of the United States thus becomes this country's foremost problem with respect to national defense.

We in the United States are fortunate that at present ours is the greatest industrial power in the world. The problem, therefore, is not to achieve a superiority we now lack but is to continue the industrial progress that has been such a striking characteristic of America's past. The continuation of this progress involves two major considerations. Immediately, we should be concerned with the day-to-day choices among alternative uses of land, labor, and capital; and, in the long run, be concerned with retaining and if possible improving the circumstances that have made great progress possible.

The Immediate Problem

Every decision to use land, labor, for one purpose use for some other purpose denies their use for some other purpose. If we build a dam in the State of Washington, for example, the decision to construct the dam prevents a certain amount of land, labor, and capital from being used in some other enterprise. This fact suggests the importance of choosing wisely among the alternative uses of land, labor, and capital.

However, the significance of making wise choices becomes especially apparent when one realizes that land, labor, and capital are not inexhaustible. There is not available so much land, labor, and capital in the United States that we may satisfy everyone's desires. The notion that whatever is desired can be done "regardless of cost" is dangerous as well as false.

In the United States the use of land, labor, and capital has been determined free-market processes. Consumers' free choice has directed the development of the present productive capacity of the United States. We believe that only through a choice among alternative uses of land, labor, and capital can the rate of industrial progress be continued.

Familiarity with possible alternatives and relative costs has led us, in our capacity as economists, to raise certain questions concerning choices that have already been made and others under consideration. When relative costs can be ascertained, the questions can be answered; when relative costs cannot be calculated, we can do no more than raise a question. Frequently, a clue to relative costs may be obtained by ascertaining whether or not the most efficient use is being made of land, labor, and capital.

Readers should remember that every expenditure of funds is in itself a choice among the alternative uses of land, labor, and capital. Readers should remember also that every unwise choice retards the rate of industrial progress.

Are Government-loan programs such as those for residential construction and those made by the Reconstruction Finance Corporation wise uses of available resources?

The basis for such Government-loan programs is to provide funds to persons and businesses unable to borrow the money elsewhere. The very principle of the program, then, is to make loans believed to be undesirable by those whose business it is to lend money. The Lustron Corporation fiasco provides an outstanding example of land, labor, and capital wasted because of a loan from the RFC. In the report of the Douglas subcommittee on monetary, credit, policies a question is raised concerning the desirability of loans to private borrowers by Government agencies. Two-thirds of the economists asked replied that such loans were undesirable. There is little doubt that the Government-loan program is hampering the Nation's industrial progress.

Is the present system of Social Security and the contemplated extension of its present provisions to cover more persons and increase payments a wise use of available land, labor, and capital?

The question might be rephrased to ask whether or not we should encourage individuals to retire at 65. In order to obtain the benefits of Social Security at 65, a worker is forced to retire even though he may have many years of productiveness to contribute. Insofar as the Social Security system eliminates effective workers from the labor force, industrial progress obviously is hampered.

Does the Government farm-support program make the most effective use of available land, labor, and capital?

Recent dumpings of potatoes emphasize the waste involved in a program that encourages excessive farm production. The land, labor, and capital embodied in the potato, eggs, butter, and other surplus commodities that are being hoarded by the Government have been almost entirely wasted. When billions of dollars' worth of land, labor, and capital are used to produce useless goods, the Nation loses in two ways: not only are the products concerned wasted, but also the Nation has been denied the use of the land, labor, and capital involved for more constructive purposes. As long as the farm program encourages the waste of land, labor, and capital, industrial progress will be retarded thereby.

Does unemployment insurance aid industrial progress?

Paying individuals for not working, at first glance, would certainly seem to be an undesirable investment. To the extent that the program encourages unemployment, there is little question that it retards industrial progress, because it denies the Nation a portion of the available labor forces. That there may be some advantages is undeniable, but certainly the notorious and widespread abuses of the unemployment-insurance program wastefully retard industrial progress.

Are the funds (that is, the land, labor, and capital represented by them) being made available to other nations through the Economic Cooperation Administration, the Atlantic Pact, and Point IV thus being used most effectively?

Of course, the billions of dollars worth of land, labor, and capital being given to other countries are lost to the United States. Every machine shipped to some other country has embodied in it land, labor, and capital that are denied to industries here. The long-term increase in industrial production in the United States during recent decades has been at an annual rate of only 3 percent; but the $5,000,000,000 we have given away to other nations in each of the last two years represents a gift of about 3 percent of the gross national product (excluding services and Government purchases of goods and services.)

Conclusions

The questions that have been raised and the answers that have been given suggest that at present we are not choosing as wisely as we could among the alternative uses of land, labor, and capital. Because these decisions are vital to the maintenance of the industrial superiority of the United States and therefore vital to the maintenance of an adequate national defense, we suggest that a reappraisal of plans and projects is in order.

Our Greatest Threat

T HE URGENT DESIRABILITY of restoring and maintaining conditions conducive to rapid industrial progress here in the United States have been overlooked. Responsible statesmen instead have been preoccupied with more striking problems such as the Marshall Plan, Atlantic Pact aid, Point IV, and other even more grandiose methods of buying national security. However, in spite of the vast propaganda urging foreign aid and in spite of such arguments as President Truman's to the effect that the Marshall Plan is cheaper than a shooting war, we are convinced that maintaining or preferably increasing the industrial superiority of the United States is the keystone in the arch of national defense.

The outstanding threat to future industrial progress is the current trend away from the degree of economic freedom that characterized the Nation's earlier development.

Apparently, one of the country's major problems is to differentiate between measures that increase and those that decrease economic freedom. When the President of the United States believes that no economic freedom has been lost by farmers who are permitted to vote for or against acceptance of production restrictions established by the Government, reconsideration of the implications and significance freedom would seem to be necessary.

Questions To Be Raised

As a means of focusing attention on the more important problems, we raise and attempt to answer certain questions in the paragraphs that follow. These questions concern not only the policies of the Federal Government but also those of other important groups in the economy.

Are industrial monopolies destroying economic freedom and retarding industrial progress?

Monopolies may prevent the most effective functioning of the market through the arbitrary manipulation of prices. Of course, the distortion of market relationships ordinarily results in a less effective use of land, labor, and capital than would otherwise occur. Probably the best procedure is to continue to fight the more obvious business monopolies, but to remember that size alone is not the criterion of monopoly.

Has the increase in the power of labor unions resulted in the lessening of economic freedom and hampered industrial progress?

On frequent occasions in the recent past the opportunity to develop natural resources or make use of capital has been denied because of strikes. Such denials in the steel, coal, automobile, and railroad industries have resulted in the wasting of natural resources, labor, and capital.

When one remembers that industrial growth in the United States during the last few decades has been at the rate of only 3 percent per annum, the importance of weeks or months of idleness in a major industry becomes apparent. Until the bargaining power of the two groups, labor and management, is more nearly equal, genuine collective bargaining is not to be expected.

And, until conditions are such as to assure the economic freedom of both parties and thus encouraging genuine collective bargaining, the national defense probably will be weakened by prolonged industrial warfare.

Is the existence of every monopoly privilege a denial of economic freedom, and does it discourage industrial progress?

Monopoly privileges enable the holders thereof to receive a portion of the Nation's product without contributing to the productive processes. For example, large fertile areas in the Midwest, as well as immensely valuable lands in many major cities are owned by present members of the British aristocracy because more than 150 years ago George III, then King of England, by a stroke of his pen, gave certain ancestors of these persons authority to hold that land forever. To the extent that special privileges of this type are perpetuated, freedom is denied to those who produce wealth on these lands and share it with the holders of the monopoly privileges.

Moreover, the slow effects on industrial progress are substantial. In the first place, the potential labor of those persons who live on the bounty provided by special privilege is lost, thereby reducing the Nation's output of goods and services. In the second place, those persons who have no special privileges but who do contribute labor or capital are forced to give part of what they produce without any return; consequently, the incentive to produce is not so great as it might otherwise be.

Government Policies
Do tariffs lessen economic freedom?

The so-called "protective tariffs" have long reduced the degree of economic freedom. In an effort to protect certain domestic industries from the competition of more efficient foreign industries, tariffs have been placed on incoming goods. One effect of "protecting" domestic industry is to perpetuate relatively inefficient uses of land, labor, and capital. Not only are land, labor, and capital thus wasted but also their use in new or more efficient industries is prevented or delayed.

Are high taxes promoting economic freedom?

There is little question that high taxes prevent the producer from receiving his production or its equivalent in value. Consequently, the expansion of production and productive facilities is discouraged. Moreover, to the extent that the Government uses the funds unwisely (for example, in making loans to such organizations as the Lustron Corporation), there is a misuse of savings that prevents the most effective expansion of the Nation's capital plant and equipment.

Does the farm price-support program lessen economic freedom?

The support program lessens economic freedom in three ways. First, free markets are distorted as demand is artificially and arbitrarily influenced by Government funds. Second, the farmer is singled out to receive special privileges. Third, the disturbance of market relationships makes the measurement of values difficult, with resulting misapplication of land, labor, and capital.

Do the monetary, credit, and fiscal policies of the Government lessen economic freedom?

The amount of inflationary purchasing media in circulation at present, largely as a result of the Government's monetary, credit, and fiscal policies exceeds $70,000,000,000. Moreover, changes in the amount of inflationary purchasing media are occurring from month to month. That this inflationary purchasing media have distorted market relationships can be seen in the great increase during the past few years in dollar wages, dollar prices, dollar profits, dollar value of construction, etc. The effects of these distortions in a capitalistic economy are far reaching. The Nation may be dissipating its capital plant and equipment without any realization of the fact by the great majority of its citizens.

When individuals speak of the gains in gross national product and in national income and must explain that they are not speaking in terms of dollars but in terms of real product and real income, the Nation's citizens should give the situation some serious thought. When the basic measure of a nation's goods and services (in the United States this measure is the dollar, one thirty-fifth of an ounce of gold) can no longer be used to measure the value of its goods and services, the time has come for that nation "to put its house in order" if disaster is to be avoided.

Conclusions

We are convinced that the greatest threat to the security of the United States is the retardation of industrial progress. Continued divergence from the principles and circumstances that have made possible the vast industrial development of the United States will hinder progress here as the technological advance has been retarded in France by four decades of inflation and monetary depreciation and in England by monopoly and "creeping" socialism.

The United States already has diverged so far from the path toward economic freedom that vast amounts of land, labor, and capital have been and are being wasted. Further divergence from freedom toward socialism may so lessen the Nation's industrial superiority as to invite attack from Russia and her satellites.

In order to preserve and defend the United States during the foreseeable future, the path toward economic freedom must be regained. Public attention should be focused on the ways and means of restoring and preserving the circumstances that have made this country great. Much effort will be required, hard work, clear thought, and accurate scientific analysis. The task will not be done in one year or ten; but, unless it is done, a succession of Marshall Plans and other aid programs will hasten rather than delay our ultimate defeat. If Western Civilization, the hope of mankind, is to be saved, it will be not by our bounty but by our example. Our first problem is to save ourselves from the consequences of numerous past and present follies, and on that aspect of our defense problem the work has barely begun.

About the Author

EDWARD C. HARWOOD (October 28, 1900 – December 16, 1980) was an economist who founded the American Institute for Economic Research (AIER) in 1933. Harwood graduated from the U.S. Military Academy in 1920. He went on to attend Rensselaer Polytechnic Institute (RPI) before being appointed an Assistant Professor of Military Science and Tactics at Massachusetts Institute of Technology (MIT) in Cambridge, MA. While at MIT, Harwood became interested in economics, particularly money-credit problems, and began an intensive study on the topic. With the encouragement of MIT Vice President Vannevar Bush, Harwood founded AIER in 1933 to provide independent research to the public on current economic conditions.

Index

Made in the USA
Lexington, KY
11 December 2019

58426571R00075